WINE

on

TUESDAYS

WINE

on

TUESDAYS

BE A SERIOUS WINE
DRINKER WITHOUT TAKING
WINE TOO SERIOUSLY

DEBRA & KEITH GORDON

THOMAS NELSON

Since 1798

NASHVILLE   DALLAS   MEXICO CITY   RIO DE JANEIRO   BEIJING

Published in Nashville, Tennessee, by Thomas Nelson. Thomas Nelson is a registered trademark of Thomas Nelson, Inc.

Thomas Nelson, Inc. titles may be purchased in bulk for educational, business, fund-raising, or sales promotional use. For information, please e-mail SpecialMarkets@ThomasNelson.com.

Permissions and Credits: Page 5, wine label reprinted with permission of Wine Library, Springfield, New Jersey. Pages 22–23, quotation from *The Emperor of Wine: The Rise of Robert M. Parker, Jr., and the Reign of American Taste* by Elin McCoy, © 2005 by Elin McCoy, published by HarperCollins. Pages 179–180, advertisement reprinted with permission of Pop's Wine and Spirits, Island Park, New York.

Illustrations on pages 188–193 by Jennifer Baldwin. All other illustrations by Kay Meadows.

Library of Congress Cataloging-in-Publication Data

Gordon, Debra L., 1962–
    Wine on Tuesdays : be a serious wine drinker without taking wine too seriously / by Debra and Keith Gordon.
        p. cm.
    Includes bibliographical references and index.
    ISBN 978-1-4016-0418-9
    1. Wine and wine making. I. Gordon, Keith, 1960–
II. Title.
TP548.G628 2008
641.2'2–dc22

                                        2008009208

Printed in the United States of America
08 09 10 11 12 — 9 8 7 6 5 4 3 2 1

To our children, Jonathan, Callum, and Iain,
for giving us the reasons we needed to begin
drinking wine in the first place

CONTENTS

CONTENTS

ACKNOWLEDGMENTS

*B*ooks are not written in a vacuum. Like a fine wine, they require time, thought, effort, and teamwork. *Wine on Tuesdays* is no exception. Our friend Lauriston Hardin is responsible for much of the work on the chapters on sparkling and dessert wines. He didn't like being edited by Debra, but then, few people do. Thanks, Lauriston, for taking it with good humor (and hope you enjoyed the case of wine you received in payment). We'd also like to thank our agent, Jeremy Katz, who found a home for the book with Thomas Nelson; Pamela Clements of Thomas Nelson for recognizing the need for such a book (and for her enthusiasm and excitement for the concept, something missing all too often in today's corporate publishing world); and Jennifer Baldwin for her great illustrations.

Thanks also to Jennifer Greenstein for her eagle editing eye (and Lauriston, if it makes you feel any better, even Deb gets edited at some point!), Sara J. Henry for her excellent copyediting skills, Kristen Vasgaard for the fabulous cover, and Kay Meadows for the beautiful text design and illustrations.

Finally, we'd like to thank the dozens of friends who introduced us to the joys of drinking wine and who have drunk so much wine with us.

INTRODUCTION

$\mathcal{T}$he evidence is clear: The United States is undergoing a wine transformation these days. Wine is starring in hit movies, taking up more shelf space in grocery stores, and even being discussed at the Supreme Court.

More important, however, wine is rapidly overtaking any other alcoholic beverage as the drink of choice among Americans. And not just cheap jug wine. Nope. Today Americans are into everything from serious French Bordeaux to fun Australian Shiraz to new varieties no one had even heard of ten years ago, such as Carménère, Mouvèdre, and Pinotage.

In the process, we're fueling a revolution. Consider these tidbits:

- In 2007, the United States' total wine consumption increased 5 percent over the previous year to 314 million cases of wine (about 3.8 *billion* bottles), the fifteenth consecutive annual increase.
- By 2015, Americans are predicted to drink more wine than the French.
- More than 7,000 brands of wine are sold in the United States.

- Wine is moving into the younger set, finding its niche with twenty- and thirtysomethings who are attracted by fun labels, screw-top caps, and the general lack of snobbiness that wine marketers are selling.
- About 13 percent of Americans drink wine two or three times a week, and 14 percent drink it occasionally, according to Adams Beverage Group.
- Women buy 60 percent of all wine sold in this country.
- Americans are red wine drinkers, with red outselling white in U.S. supermarkets for the first time in 2004.
- Our favorite wines are Chardonnay, Merlot, White Zinfandel, and Cabernet Sauvignon, which make up more than half the wines sold in supermarkets.

We're most excited about a 2005 Gallup poll in which Americans picked wine as their favorite beverage. Okay, maybe it *did* tie with beer, but hey, that's still pretty good. Consider that in the 1992 poll wine came in dead last behind beer and liquor, with less than a third of Americans calling it their favorite alcoholic beverage.

And don't think retailers haven't caught on. Heck, today some warehouse clubs and discount stores even sell their own private-labeled wines, so you don't have to spend a lot to get a lot.

One of the biggest-selling wines of this century isn't some fancy French vintage, but an everyday quaffable varietal with the nickname "Two-Buck Chuck" for its $1.99 price. Trader Joe grocery stores have sold millions of bottles of this wine—even to so-called gourmets. And the wine company Vino 100 is franchising wine stores around the country that stock 100 wines for under $25.

Hence, the name of this book: *Wine on Tuesdays*. Our goal is to show you that wine is no longer some stuffy, fusty libation best served in crystal glasses in hushed, walnut-paneled rooms. It's fun, fresh, and fantastic, meant to be drunk with everything, all the time, even on Tuesdays (which we consider the dullest day of the week). What better way to shake up spaghetti, galvanize meatloaf, and relax after a homework session with your fifth-grader than with a glass of wine?

But what we've found over the years is that many people are too intimidated by wine. Perhaps they feel that they can't drink anything but mass-produced jug wine because they "don't really understand wine." Or they view wine as only something to be served on special occasions. When they get to know us—which means drinking wine often—and start to relax, they realize that all these years they've been frightened of a ghost. Learning about wine is not complicated; heck, *wine* is not complicated. So where do these myths come from?

At the risk of creating a lot of enemies, we think it comes, to a great extent, from wine writers. Many books out there about wine are written for people who already know about wine. Pick one up and you're likely to run screaming from anything even resembling a Cabernet Sauvignon.

That's why we decided to write *Wine on Tuesdays*.

Our goal is not to teach you everything you need to know about wine. It is not to make you a wine expert. It is not to have you run out and build a wine cellar and begin talking about "futures," and "palate," and "finishes." It is to show you that drinking wine is fun, fabulous, fantastic—and to bring you into our world, where you can reach for a glass of wine with dinner as naturally as you reach for your seat belt when you get into the car. There's nothing scary about wine; what's scary are all those books and people who try to "teach" you about wine. We promise that *Wine on Tuesdays* is not such a book.

Maybe you're not convinced. Maybe you're staring into your Budweiser and wondering why you should bother to switch, still asking yourself *why* you should drink wine.

We're so glad you asked.

CHAPTER 1

WHY BOTHER WITH WINE?

*I*f there's one thing we want you to take away from this first chapter (and from this book), it's that wine is much more than just a beverage. It can add to your life in ways that extend far beyond having something nice to drink with dinner.

We've made many deep friendships through wine tastings and wine conversations. We've struck up conversations with total strangers sitting at a table next to us at a restaurant when we asked about the bottle of Côtes du Rhônes they were drinking.

We've also had some really fun times around wine, not just from drinking it. Take the Sunday afternoon we spent with our good friends Dave and Gert bottling the homemade Super Tuscan Dave makes, then eating Gert's amazing Italian feast, complete with authentic antipasti from Philadelphia's North End and a stunning California Cabernet.

Sure, dinner would have been fun regardless, but the bottling (and drinking) added an extra level of enjoyment. Which is just what wine does to an occasion—bump it up a notch.

One of our all-time favorite wine events occurred

on a crisp, late October day at the home of our friends Peggy and Jerry. They live in a renovated farmhouse on about twenty acres in the country, mostly woodlands. They love the Italian game of bocce, a type of outdoor bowling in which you try to get your team's ball to rest as close to the *pallino* ball while knocking away your competitors' balls. Every year they host a giant party/picnic on their property, complete with barbecue, bocce, and, of course, endless bottles of wine.

As the afternoon faded and the air cooled, Jerry lit the giant bonfires he had laid around the perimeter of the bocce court. We grabbed a couple of glasses and a half-empty bottle of red wine and joined some friends on a bench before a blazing fire. There we sat for more

THE TOP TEN REASONS TO DRINK WINE

With apologies to David Letterman, here are our top ten reasons to drink wine:

10. It's good for you.
9. It's a great way to make new friends.
8. It makes even an ordinary hamburger special.
7. It teaches you geography.
6. It's much sexier to sip from a beautiful glass than from a long-necked beer bottle.
5. It's the ultimate addition to a romantic evening.
4. It's possible to drink a glass at lunch and still function in the afternoon.
3. It comes in so many colors and vareties, with so many neat names.
2. It gives you a reason to buy lots of cool wine-related accessories.

And the number one reason to drink wine:

1. It just tastes so darn good.

than an hour, soaking in the scent of the wood smoke, the warmth of the wine, and the joy of the friendship. It was as close to heaven as you can get!

Or how about the three days we spent in Las Vegas attending the 2005 American Wine Society (AWS) meeting? Or the four days in Napa, California, attending a conference on Wine and Heart Health geared towards cardiologists (yeah, it was a boondoggle for them *and* us)? Talk about *fun!* And when you're in your mid-forties with one kid in college, two at home, two stressful jobs, a big house, a smelly dog, and a neurotic cat, you take your fun where you can get it.

Then there's the sense of place attached to wine. As you'll learn, wine doesn't exist in a vacuum. Behind every bottle of good wine is a vineyard lovingly planted by someone, a home, a community.

Finally, we love wine because of the history attached to it. Open a bottle of twenty-year-old Bordeaux and take a moment to imagine what the world was like when that wine was created. Why do you think so many people put down a case of wine the day their son is born, to be drunk at his wedding decades later; or put aside a couple of special bottles the day their daughter starts kindergarten, anticipating pulling them out to toast her college graduation? Wine is a connection to our past, present, and future.

MAKING WINE: THE BASICS

So now you know *why* you should drink wine. In the next chapter, we'll tell you *how* to drink wine. Now it's time to get a bit of background on just how wine is made.

If your vision of making wine has to do with the old *I Love Lucy* episode where she and Ethel stomp on the grapes, stop right there.

Making wine has two main elements: the vineyard and the vintner, or winemaker. The vineyard, of course, is where the grapes are grown. And the vintner is the person actually responsible for making the wine.

Sometimes the person making the wine is also the one overseeing the vineyard in which the grapes are grown. More often, however, they're widely separate, as many wineries buy grapes from numerous vineyards around the area, state, or even country. We know one Virginia vineyard, for instance, that ships in Zinfandel grapes from California. (After tasting the resulting wine, however, we'd suggest they stick with Virginia grapes.)

Anyway, to give you a good overview of the wine-making process, we thought we'd start with the back label from a wine we recently drank: a Sharpshooter

WINE PIONEER: ROBERT MONDAVI

Known as the father of the California wine industry, Robert Mondavi opened his own winery in 1965 after splitting from the family winery.

His fame came after he repackaged the oaky Sauvignon Blanc he created in 1968 with the sexy name Fumé Blanc (attesting to his remarkable marketing ability). Later, he joined with French wine king Baron Philippe de Rothschild of Château Mouton Rothschild in the Bordeaux region of France to create the premier wine (read: really, really expensive) Opus One. Today, Opus One is considered one of the top California wines, retailing for nearly $200 a bottle.

Cabernet Sauvignon, made in Paso Robles on California's Central Coast. We bought this wine for about $17 a few years ago. We consider it a "Friday night wine," a bit too expensive for every day, but just perfect for small celebrations, such as the end of the work week. Here's what the label says:

> The warm climate and alluvial soils of the Paso Robles area make it ideally suited to grow Cabernet Sauvignon. In keeping with Sharp-shooter standards, the grapes used in this wine were sourced entirely from two top vineyards around Paso Robles. The grapes were entirely hand-harvested in mid-October. Yields were small at 3 tons per acre. After destemming, the must was fermented using native yeasts in open-top fermenters. The wine was then transferred to both French and American oak barrels, 25% of which were new, and aged for 30 months. Drink the 2002 Sharpshooter Cabernet Sauvignon right now or cellar for up to 10 years.

Sound like a bit of Greek? Okay, we'll translate, because this description provides a great overview of winemaking and wine in general.

> The warm climate and alluvial soils of the Paso Robles area make it ideally suited to grow Cabernet Sauvignon.

Although wine grapes are grown all over the world in every possible climate (even Alaska!), varietals such

WHAT DOES IT MEAN?

When people talk about making wine, you may hear some other terms thrown around. Here's your primer:

Brix: Sugar content of the wine.

Aging: How long the wine spent after fermentation before bottling. Aging usually occurs in wooden barrels or stainless steel casks.

Malolactic (secondary) fermentation: A separate special fermentation that leads to a softer, mellower wine.

Racking: Siphoning off the clear juice from the sediment that falls to bottom of the wine container. May be done naturally or with certain additives, like cream of tartar.

There, now no one will know that the closest you've been to a vineyard is your Uncle Harry's grape arbor.

as Cabernet Sauvignon tend to do best in places with long warm, even hot, spells and mild winters. That's why California is the Cabernet king. This is particularly true in the inland valleys of the Central Coast and Northern California, where the hot days of summer are tempered by cool breezes off the Pacific. Meanwhile, winters are mild and late frosts—once the vines have set their buds—rare.

Now, those alluvial soils. *Alluvial* means sediment deposited by flowing waters. In other words, the soils of the vineyards were once the banks or even beds of streams and rivers. Why is this important? One word, my friend: *terroir*, which means "earth" in French, but much more in "winespeak." True wine connoisseurs believe that grapes in a vineyard pick up the flavors of the soil in which they're grown, one of many reasons why every year's wine, also called the vintage, is different.

You'll often hear terroir referred to when describing the taste of a certain wine, as in, "This Chardonnay is reminiscent of the rocky limestone terroir in which it was grown." We once tasted an amazing Cabernet Sauvignon from Chile that tasted like mint. Why? The land on which the vines were grown had once been host to a grove of eucalyptus trees.

That's also why the label on this bottle tells you that

> the grapes used in this wine were sourced entirely
> from two top vineyards around Paso Robles.

In other words, "We didn't just buy a trainload of grapes from down south and throw 'em in the crusher." This winemaker likely spends a great deal of time scouting vineyards in the area, tasting the grapes, the resulting wine, and even the soil to find the grapes and conditions deemed ideal for the winery's production. This level of care and attention is just one of several reasons behind this bottle's $17 price tag compared to the $7 you'd pay for a mass-produced wine, in which the majority of grapes were purchased based on price, not quality.

START WITH THE GRAPE

Wine starts, of course, with the grapes. As you'll learn in this book, the most popular grapes for winemaking are the basic six varietals (a varietal is the type of grape used to make the wine): chardonnay, sauvignon blanc, cabernet sauvignon, merlot, zinfandel, and pinot noir. Of course, there are literally hundreds of other grapes and you'll learn more about some of them in later chapters, but for now we'll stick with the basics.

Growing grapes and making wine is not for the impatient. From the time you plant the first vines, it takes at least three years before you can harvest the grapes for your first wine, and anywhere from another year to three or more before the wine is ready for bottling and its journey to the retail store.

Why so long? Grapevines are a finicky lot. For one, they tend to grow best in the worst soil. Rocky, poor soil that is not much good for growing anything else tends to be best for vines. The worse the soil, the harder the vine has to work to get water and nutrients. That means it sends its root system deep, deep into the ground, giving new meaning to the expression "putting down roots." The deeper and further into the soil the roots go, the more root surface is available to take in the nutrients and character of the soil itself. You already know what character is, right? Right. It's the terroir.

HARVESTING THE GRAPES
Back to our wine label:

> The grapes were entirely hand-harvested in mid-October. Yields were small at 3 tons per acre.

Okay, what this tells you is that these people are serious about their grapes. They didn't send some mechanical picker into the fields to sweep the grapes up; instead, they hired workers—lots of workers—to walk up and down the rows and gently snip each bunch of fruit from the vine. The fact that yields were small means the grapes they did get were likely high in sugar, making them sweeter and richer and creating a more powerful wine for us.

This is all very important. One of the great things about wine is its variety. Two bottles of wine from the same vineyard and winery but from different years can taste entirely different. Why? Maybe one year saw more sun and less rain; the owner decided to pick the grapes a little later; or the farm workers did a better job plucking leaves off the vines in the early spring so more sun could warm the grapes, increasing their sugar content. The higher the sugar content, the stronger the wine, in both taste and alcohol level.

Similarly, the winery may have changed winemakers. The new winemaker may prefer aging the wine in new French oak barrels, instead of American oak barrels. Or perhaps the old winemaker let the grapes ferment for an extra day or two, or used some unique combination of yeast and other additives to bring it to perfect fruition.

Bottom line: Wine is one of the few things left in this packaged world that relies on a unique combination of nature, individual talent, taste, and—most of all—luck to create a unique product.

As they say, variety really *is* the spice of life!

FROM GRAPE TO WINE

After destemming, the must was fermented using native yeasts in open-top fermenters.

Once the grapes reach their ultimate ripeness (the peak of their sweetness), the rest is fairly simple. The grapes are picked (either by hand or machine) and thrown into a machine called, appropriately enough, the crusher. About the size of a low-end gas grill, the crusher uses a metal, corkscrew-like apparatus to pulverize the grapes, spitting out seeds and stems (and bugs and sticks and the old sock someone left in the vineyard) onto the ground, while juice and skins gush through a large hose at more than a gallon a minute into tanks or, as we saw at one small winery, oversized garbage pails. What's left is called the *must*, the juice of freshly crushed grapes, which may include some seeds and skin.

If you're making white wine, you then drain off the juice and allow it to ferment. Fermentation is when the natural yeasts on grape skins turn sugar to alcohol. If you're making red wine, you leave the juice in contact with the skins, which is where the color comes from. The longer the contact, the deeper the color. So, if you're making a rosé, the contact between the two might be just a week; for a red Zinfandel, it might be a month or more.

Regardless, the fermentation process is the same with red or white wines: Yeast cells on the grape skins get washed into the juice itself or added by the wine-maker, where a complex chemical process (the same that leads to that crusty loaf of sourdough bread) begins. The yeast gradually turns the sugars in the grapes into alcohol and, voila! A wine is born.

AGING THE WINE

Of course, you wouldn't want to drink the plonk that emerges in the first few days of fermentation. So you let it age for months, years, or, in the case of high-end wines, decades. As our label says:

The wine was then transferred to both French and American oak barrels, 25% of which were new, and aged for 30 months.

In our somewhat simplified version of winemaking, this is the final step before bottling. Wine is typically stored in either oak barrels or stainless steel tanks, depending on the winemaker's preference and the type of wine. You can bet that if it's stored in oak barrels, particularly French oak barrels, it's going to be a higher-priced wine. Each of those barrels costs more than $600—and some winemakers use them just once!

Oak is big in the wine business, particularly in American wines and those made especially for the American market. Seems we like the vanilla flavor oak imparts to a wine, so much so that less expensive wines that aren't aged in oak barrels are sometimes filtered through oak chips or dust to impart the same smoky flavor at a much lower price.

BOTTLES AND CORKS

The final step is getting the wine into a container, typically a bottle, and closing it off with a cork. While that's still how the majority of wines are packaged today, the times are a-changin'.

From sparkling wines in cans to high-quality wines bottled with screw caps, the message is clear: Forget about judging the quality of the wine by its packaging.

One of the hottest debates in the wine world these days is over corks versus alternate closures. With the image of cheap, fortified wine (think Thunderbird and MD 20/20), the idea of a screw top on a fine wine makes many purveyors shudder. But, say proponents, if you've ever opened a $50 bottle of wine only to find that it smells like the wet socks your thirteen-year-old left in the back of the van one hot August afternoon, a screw top looks pretty good.

About one out of twenty wines has a cork tainted with a dastardly chemical called TCA, the abbreviation for the chemical compound 2,4,6-trichloroanisole. TCA is formed as the result of a complex chemical reaction involving certain chemicals in cork. If it forms, the wine is considered "corked," and it tastes and smells rotten. If you get a corked bottle, you can always return it to the store where you purchased it. But that's a pain.

Switch to a screw top, however, and there's no risk of corkage. We've even found a great, drinkable French Bordeaux that sells for about $10 a bottle with a screw top. Hey, if the French are moving to screw tops, you know they're becoming accepted in the wine world.

One concern: How will the wine age with a screw top as compared to a traditional cork? The few experiments conducted so far show pretty well. Why else would PlumpJack winery of Oakville, California (whose wines routinely sell for upward of $60 a bottle), have started putting screw tops on its exclusive Reserve Cabernet Sauvignon? The screw caps work so well that within a few years, experts say, nearly all wines under $30—and quite a few over—will be sporting them.

Winemakers do have other options. More are using synthetic corks made from plastic to seal their bottles. This also works well and removes the worry about corkage. And recently we've begun seeing ingenious glass corks, particularly on Italian wines trying to differentiate themselves in a crowded market. These corks look like decanter stoppers and are so lovely Deb wanted to drill a hole in one and string it on a chain to wear around her neck.

Of course, you could do away with the whole bottle-and-stopper idea altogether and use entirely different packaging for your wine, which many winemakers are doing.

CARTONS AND BAGS—OH, MY!

Keith spent three years in Australia getting his Ph.D. in reproductive physiology (and spending more time than he'd like to remember with wallabies and kangaroos). Small wonder, then, that he also drank a lot of wine.

Without telling you Keith's age, let's just say that it was so long ago that few outside the country had ever heard of Australian wine. In the big country, however, its citizens found drinking really good Shiraz or Chardonnay from a box no odder than celebrating Christmas in the midst of summer.

For the Australians learned early on what we're just coming to understand. Put five gallons of wine in an airtight bag that collapses every time a glass is poured and the wine retains its quality for weeks. Not to mention it's darn convenient when you've got a crowd. Today, slightly more than half of all wine in Australia is sold in boxes, compared to about 18 percent (or one in five glasses) in the United States.

Back in the States, however, we were used to thinking of wine-in-a-box as simply another name for rotgut-in-a-box. It took another twenty years before we caught on. Today you can find some excellent, drinkable, everyday wines packaged in boxes.

One of the hottest is Ryan Sproule's Black Box wine (packaged, of course, in a black box) whose elegant container holds about three gallons of high-end wine—Chardonnay, Cabernet, Merlot, and Shiraz—and sells for about $25. Next time you have a party, pick up a few boxes and watch your guests' faces as they take the first sip, expecting alcoholic grape juice but finding a really good drinking wine. Priceless.

BEYOND BOXES

If you don't want the equivalent of four bottles of wine but need some portable wine for a picnic or road trip (not drinking *on* the road, of course), try the newest in wine packaging: cartons, plastic bottles, and glasses.

The cartons are called Tetra Paks and are the same containers that hold shelf-stable milk or chicken stock. They contain about three glasses of wine (a 750 milliliter bottle holds about four) and are eminently portable.

If you want just a little wine to go with your PB&J at lunch, try the small plastic bottles just turning up on grocery store shelves. These miniature bottles hold about six ounces and come in four packs. Stone Cellars, a division of wine giant Beringer, sells a pack of twenty-four single servings for about $47.

Of course, even if you buy those portable wine packages, you still need a glass. Wouldn't it be nice if you could find something on store shelves that *included* the glass? Enter the Tulipak, a biodegradable plastic glass filled with 6.3 ounces of wine hermetically

BLACK BOX WINE

Why buy a box rather than a glass? We like to keep a box in the fridge for those times when we want just one glass, say, with lunch on a weekend, or as a final nightcap, without opening a new bottle. It's also a great bargain. The Australian Banrock Station, for instance, retails for about $7 a bottle; buy it in the 3-liter box and the price drops to the equivalent of about $4 a bottle, about a 75 percent savings.

Most boxed wine is sold in three-liter containers; each holds the equivalent of about four standard 750-milliliter wine bottles. Inside the box, a triple-layer plastic airtight bag contains the wine. Pouring is easy: Just poke a hole in the bottom, pull out the plastic spout, and push the button. While manufacturers say the wine remains fresh for about four weeks, we find it keeps much longer—up to six months in some cases if refrigerated.

sealed with aluminum like a small juice bottle. Al Fresco Wines is selling the glasses filled with Australian Chardonnay, Shiraz, and rosé in the United Kingdom. We figure it's only a matter of time before they turn up on U.S. store shelves.

THE ADVENTURE AWAITS

Now that you've got the wine basics down—or at least know enough not to cringe when your host unscrews the cap from that tempting Pinot Noir—it's time to move deeper into the wine world.

For the next chapter, we strongly advise that you get yourself a bottle and a glass. This is where it gets fun!

CHAPTER 2

SMELL AND TASTE: FINDING YOUR OWN PALATE

*B*efore you start this chapter, you're going to need some supplies. So pull out a couple of wine glasses (more on the glasses themselves in Chapter 12), and grab a couple of bottles of the magic grape: one white, one red. It doesn't matter what type or what brand, just a wine you enjoy drinking.

Because in this chapter, you're going to meet your palate. What's that, you ask? It's the way the wine feels and tastes in your mouth. But palates are not born. Oh, no. Palates are developed over time and with experience. That means you have to drink a lot of wine! (It's a rough job, but someone has to do it.) Palates also differ dramatically from person to person. It's why Keith loves minerally Chardonnays and Debra loves buttery Chardonnays.

If you get nothing else out of this chapter, remember this: Taste is subjective. It's why you love chocolate and your sister loves crème caramel. And nowhere is taste more subjective than when it comes to wine. The greatest wine expert in the world could absolutely hate a particular wine that you love. Does it make that wine bad? Not to you.

Here's a good example. At our first wine event, a Bordeaux tasting, about twenty-five people (none of whom we knew) were seated around a table. As each wine was poured and tasted, the host (who was a super wine snob) went around the table asking each person to describe the wine and give their opinion. There was *never* a consensus, not on any of the thirteen wines we tried that day.

Invariably, about a third of the table loved the wine, a third pronounced it just "so-so," and a third absolutely hated it. We learned a valuable lesson that day: If the quality of art is in the eye of the beholder, then the quality of wine is in the palate of the drinker.

And thus we come to the ten commandments of wine tasting:

1. Thou shalt always sniff first.
2. Thou shalt know that there are no rules when it comes to tasting wine.
3. Thou must respect everyone's palate, for all are different.
4. Thy palate changes with the day, the hour, the food, the company, and the location.
5. Thou must be adventurous.
6. Thy first impression is usually right.
7. Thou shalt not view the label whilst tasting.
8. Thou shalt not consider the price whilst tasting.
9. Thou shalt not be ashamed of liking something no one else does (which could mean a good price on the wine).
10. Thou shalt taste wine in large glasses.

OPENING THE WINE

Before you start tasting you have to open that darn bottle. Unless you're imbibing from the aforementioned box, can, Tetra Pak, and so on, or unless your bottle is closed with a screw cap, that means decorking.

In Chapter 12, we describe several types of wine openers and how to use them. For today's lesson, we're going to start with the very basic wing corkscrew. We have about six at our house because every time we go out of town and buy a bottle of wine for our hotel room, we realize once again we forgot to bring a corkscrew. So we buy yet another of these ubiquitous instruments, available at any grocery store.

First, look at the top of the bottle of wine. Usually foil, paper, or wax is wrapped around the cork. Using scissors, the sharp tip of the "screw" part of your wine opener, or a knife, carefully cut the foil and peel it away.

Now place the bottom "cap" of the corkscrew (the part that looks like a little hat) on top of the cork, gently working the tip of the auger (the part with the spirals) into the cork. Holding this part of the corkscrew steady with your left hand (assuming you're right handed), begin twisting the handle of the corkscrew clockwise. The auger should slowly enter the cork as the "wings" on either side of the corkscrew rise up. Continue twisting until you can't see any spirals, then, with both hands, pull the wings down.

The cork should pop out easily. To remove the cork from the corkscrew, twist the cork in the opposite direction and place it aside.

TO BREATHE OR NOT TO BREATHE?

Now that you've got the wine open, you have to ask yourself a very crucial question: Does my wine need to breathe? Actually, let's start with an even more crucial question: Why would *any* wine need to breathe?

The best way to answer that question is with a little experiment. Take your red wine and pour about two inches into two glasses. Take a sip of the glass on the left following the tasting instructions outlined in this chapter. What do you taste? Is it soft, tannic (makes your mouth pucker)? Is it astringent (makes you wrinkle your nose)? Write down your thoughts.

Now go clean the kitchen or fold laundry or walk the dog or pay your taxes. Come back in about an hour and try the second glass of wine. Notice a difference? We'll bet you do. Maybe the wine that tasted strong and robust an hour earlier now tastes as weak as your great-aunt's forearms. Or, conversely, maybe the wine that was so tannic it puckered your mouth has evolved into one with velvety softness, reminding you of thick custards and chocolate-covered cherries.

The reason for either change in flavor is the same: oxygen. Oxygen is one of the most reactive molecules around. It's the reason metal rusts, silver tarnishes, and apples brown. It's also the reason we have wine in the first place. Without oxygen's ability to jump-start complex chemical reactions in basic grapes and grape juice, we'd never get to fermentation and, ultimately, the ideal Pinot Noir.

But like any powerful element, oxygen has its downside. Too much oxygen in a wine—whether during production or while in the bottle—and you wind up with purple water. Too little, and the wine is as tight as a southern belle's corset.

That's the idea behind the whole aging thing. Even though your wine is safely secluded behind the glass and cork of the bottle and stopper, some oxygen is still seeping in, slowly continuing that magical chemical reaction that turns tight tannins into smooth chocolate flavors with a bit of leather that seems to go on and on. (More on aging in Chapter 13.)

Letting a wine "breathe," then, is like giving it a quick bit of aging. That's why whenever we open a bottle that we don't like, we usually set it aside for a day to see what happens once the wine has "opened" and breathed a bit. Usually we still don't like it and it goes on the cooking wine shelf, but occasionally we'll find a hidden gem.

Back to the original question: Does your wine need to breathe? In most instances, no (much to the chagrin of Keith, who has this very cool decanter in which the wine runs along the sides of the glass to insure optimal aeration). Keith doesn't get to play with his toy very often because most wines are drinkable the minute the cork comes out of the bottle.

And some wines—particularly older wines—definitely shouldn't be decanted because all the flavor might disappear up the neck of the decanter like smoke up a chimney.

In general, all you need to do is open a bottle about fifteen to thirty minutes before you're ready to drink.

If, however, you have a bottle of extremely rich, strong, tannic wine—a wine that seems to have enough legs to grab its own bottle and walk away from you—or a very "tight" wine (described on page 31), why, then, thirty minutes to an hour of "breathing" in the bottle or even via a decanter is a good idea.

You may also want to decant if the wine has a layer of sediment at the bottom. This is perfectly safe (if a bit gritty), but to avoid it in the final glass, you can decant the wine, keeping the sediment in the bottle, and pour it from the decanter.

Finally, a good reason to let a wine breathe in the glass or a decanter is to blow off vegetal aromas. Some whites, for instance, can have volatiles, acetone or cat pee–type smells, that dissipate quickly once they're exposed to air.

And if you're wondering if wine can "breathe" while still in the bottle, the answer is not much. There's just not enough contact between the wine and the oxygen to make much of a difference. You're better off pouring it into a big bowled glass and swirling.

LEARNING TO TASTE

In her book, *The Emperor of Wine*, a biography of wine critic Robert Parker, author Erin McCoy describes how Parker tastes the more than 100 wines he sniffs, swallows, and spits several days of the week:

> The method was precise. He picked up a glass, eyed the color, swirled the glass briskly, sniffed the wine, focused on it. The smell was the most important factor, the taste only a confirmation of that. He took a large sip, sucked in air over the liquid through pursed lips, quietly gurgling as he worked

it around his tongue, almost chewing it, and held it
in his mouth for a few seconds; then he unceremoniously spat it out into the sink.

Right about now you're rolling your eyes and
going, "See, this is why I stick with beer." Okay, okay.
Maybe the whole tasting thing can get a bit out of
hand, but it's a necessary step if you ever find yourself
at an official wine tasting, get into wine travel and visit
wineries, or want to educate your palate. We promise
that if you don't want to suck, gurgle, or spit, you don't
have to. But it's still a good idea to understand the
thinking behind the process of tasting.

We're going to teach you how to taste by focusing
on four of your five senses: sight, smell, taste, and feel.

TAKE A GOOD LOOK

Start with how the wine looks. Ideally, hold your
glass up against a white tablecloth or counter. Then
describe what you see. Don't overthink any of this—
just write or say the first words that pop into your head.

For white wines, for instance, that word probably
won't be "white." Because white wines really aren't
white. Instead, they fall somewhere upon a continuum
of gold, from pale, almost straw gold that is nearly clear
to a deep golden yellow that seems to glow from within.

What's really fun is to take two glasses of the same
type of wine and compare them. The other night Keith
poured two Gewürztraminers: one a pale straw color,
the other the color of springtime honey. The tastes,
oddly enough, matched the color. The first was lighter,
slightly astringent, with lingering notes of banana and

caramel and a bit of effervescence. The second was pure honey, meltingly heavy on the tongue.

Red wines fall somewhere along a continuum of pale rose to dark purple. Want to impress your friends and wine-drinking buddies? Make a cheat sheet from paint chips, with their fifty ways to describe "red." After all, purple is boring; but magenta is not. Pink is dull, but pale cranberry pops. Think about the red of a poppy versus the red of Georgia clay. Or the gold of a New Year's Eve party favor versus the gold of the setting sun, the yellow of butter versus the yellow of a rain slicker. You get the picture (pun intended).

Now slightly tilt your glass and watch the wine slide down the sides, leaving traces along the side of the glass like the silvery trail a snail leaves as it moves along your garden path.

These trails are known as the "legs" of the wine. Unlike Marilyn Monroe's legs, however, these legs are more than just another pretty feature. They represent the alcohol content; the higher the alcohol content, the longer the legs take to run down the glass.

TIME FOR THE NOSE

Your next step is to start swirling. Why? Swirling exposes more of the wine to oxygen, helps the alcohol evaporate, and releases molecules of scent into the air.

Now it's time to smell.

Okay, you're thinking, *I thought this was a wine tasting. What's with all the smelling?*

To answer that question, think about the last time you had a cold and how your food tasted. Or *didn't* taste. Our sense of taste is enormously influenced by our sense

DON'T MAKE THIS MISTAKE!

Skip the perfume, cologne, scented deodorant, and soaps when tasting wine. And never, ever, light a scented candle. The competing smells play havoc with your ability to tease out the aromas in the wine.

of smell. In fact, our nose is about a thousand times more sensitive than our mouth.

So close your eyes, stick your nose deep into the glass, inhale deeply, and hold it. Tilt your head back and try to connect the smells with memories. Keith grew up in Scotland where kids drank gallons of the black currant juice Ribena. Today, he often picks up black currant in red wines. Debra, on the other hand, has no clue what black currant smells like.

So where does the aroma take you? To the field behind your best friend's house? To the kitchen where your mother made chocolate cake? To the smell of your uncle's pipe tobacco as he expounded on his war exploits? Nothing carries us back to our past like scent. This is also a good way to remember a wine; the next time you see this wine, you'll recall that it made you think of the scent of the shore during your annual beach vacation or the vanilla cookies your grandmother baked at Christmas.

Okay, enough wandering down memory lane. Time to document what you smell. First ask yourself if your nose feels like it's burning. If so, then you just got an important clue about the wine—it's high in alcohol.

It's also quite possible that you smell nothing, or very little. If this happens, set the glass down and announce,

"I'm not getting much on the nose." Everyone will think you really know what you're talking about. And you do, in a way: You've just described the *intensity* of the aroma and, obviously, it's very weak. Other words to describe it are medium, aromatic, and very aromatic (descriptive, aren't they?).

Now consider the *quality* of the aroma. Was this wine born on the wrong side of the tracks or did it go to Harvard? Here's where words such as simple, ordinary, agreeable, disagreeable, complex, and elegant come into play. What do they mean? Exactly what you think they mean—this isn't rocket science.

Now we get to the fun part: using concrete words to describe the scent. Hopefully by now the scent has woken up your olfactory nerve, sending lightning-fast signals to the more developed part of your brain, the part responsible for speech and words. And that part is now sending descriptors your way.

Many new wine drinkers say even if they *can* smell something, they have no idea how to describe what they're smelling. Relax. It takes practice (and that's the fun part!).

Luckily, there's also a widely used cheat sheet: the Wine Aroma Wheel, developed by University of California–Davis enologist (pronounced *ee*-nologist) Ann C. Noble, Ph.D.

"Dr. Ann," as she's called, was a sensory chemist and professor in the department of viticulture and enology when she had the brilliant idea of creating a common language for wine lovers to describe the olfactory sensations of wine.

She dipped into her research funds to develop the Wine Aroma Wheel, publishing it in 1984 and copyrighting it in 1990, with all initial proceeds going for further wine research.

Dr. Noble, now a professor emeritus, retired in 2002 and today is a consultant to the industry. She's started taking some of those wine wheel profits for herself (well-deserved, too) and has had the wheel translated into seven languages. You can purchase your own plastic wine wheel, available in several colors and seven languages in addition to English, at www.winearomawheel.com.

Her wheel is composed of three tiers, with the terms for describing the wine becoming more specific as you move from the inner to the outer tier. The inner tier might describe an aroma as "fruity," while the outer tier would give you choices like grapefruit, strawberry, or pineapple.

Generally, with a white wine you're talking fruity, grassy, or vegetal odors. You'd use words such as pineapple, citrusy, or even buttery to describe the aroma. Wait, you're saying, wouldn't these also be the same words I use to describe the taste? Yes, indeedy. Again, recall the tremendous effect your nose has on your taste.

With red wines, you're still getting fruit, but instead of citrusy, it's likely to be more berry-like, as in strawberry, raspberry, boysenberry, or Keith's black currants. You'll also get peppery aromas, chocolaty aromas, even the scent of tobacco (think pipe tobacco), or molasses. We'll talk more about these in later chapters.

FINALLY—TIME TO TASTE!

Okay. Now it's time to taste. Fill your mouth partway with a sip of the wine. Now do what your mother always told you not to do when eating soup: Swish it around your mouth. *Gently!* This isn't mouthwash.

DON'T TASTE ALONE

There's no better way to taste wine than with a wine tasting. It doesn't have to be complicated. To plan a wine tasting:

1. Pick a day and time. We recommend between 4:00 and 5:00 p.m. so there's plenty of time for dinner after.
2. Invite about twelve friends.
3. Choose the wines and enclose them in numbered paper bags.
4. About an hour before your guests arrive, open the wines.
5. At each place, have a wine rating form and pen, and at least two wine glasses plus a water glass.
6. Put out baskets of bread or crackers and pitchers of water.
7. Place a spit bucket in the middle of each table for the spitters amongst you.
8. Pour one or two wines at a time.
9. Taste!
10. After each taste, talk about the wine. Describe what it looked like, what you smelled, what you tasted, what you liked, what you didn't.

The swishing or swirling further aerates the wine and allows it to reach every corner of your mouth and, thus, taste buds (try not to dribble; definitely *not* cool).

HOW DOES IT FEEL?

This is also when you get the "mouthfeel" of the wine. Obviously, it's the way the wine feels in your mouth. Think about how liquids feel in your mouth. Water, for instance, is very, very light, whereas milk is heavy and creamy. Wine, too, has a certain mouthfeel. It could be light, like water, syrupy (common in dessert wines or sweet Rieslings), velvety (typical for Merlots or Pinot Noirs), or even oily.

If you're a spitter, now is the time to spit. We're not

suggesting you spit; generally, it's only for professional wine tasters who sample upward of 100 wines a day. If they didn't spit, they'd be on the floor by lunchtime. And by the time you've smelled, sipped, and swished, you've hit all the major high points necessary to determine the flavor and quality of a wine.

We've only had to resort to spitting once, while attending the American Wine Society's (AWS) national conference in Las Vegas. The days began with a champagne breakfast at 8:00 a.m. and continued on through four classes (all with full tastings), cocktail hour, dinner (with about eight wines on the table), and then the hospitality suite until 2:00 a.m., so the only way to survive was by spitting. Usually, however, we swallow.

Okay, let's assume you're the swallowing type. You swallow the wine. Now describe it. Don't try to overintellectualize this; think of it as a kind of sensory Rorschach test. Just say the first words that come into your mind.

Need some help? Here's our cheat sheet for wine tasting:

Aggressive. This is a wine that, as we say in our house, reaches up, pulls you down, and gives you the kind of intense kiss destined to get your knees shaking. It's powerful and in-your-face.

Acidic. Acids are important in wine. They help maintain its structure and let it age. The acidity in a wine—particularly white wines—render them crisp and refreshing. Without acids, you'd call a wine flabby, described later in this list. An acidic wine might also be called crisp.

Austere. This wine dresses in cream-colored linen sheaths and dines only on crustless cucumber sandwiches or a single lettuce leaf with five perfect grapes.

This is a wine for an elegant occasion, a wine that holds its head high (maybe too high). Think French whites and sparkling wines like champagne.

Balanced. The same things that make a meal, a room, or an outfit balanced make a wine balanced. Namely, having all the correct elements in place. That would be acidity, fruitiness, alcohol, and tannins. No one element overpowers any other. A balanced wine is also said to have a strong backbone.

Complex. Well, complexity is always in the eyes of the beholder. To us, preparing a dinner party for ten people is pretty simple; to others, cooking a meatloaf for two is stunningly complex. But generally, a complex wine is one that has layers of flavors that seem to open up as you drink it. This is also a wine that will age well. (More on aging in Chapter 13.)

Dry. How can a liquid be dry? Easy. If it's not sweet, it's considered dry.

Fat. No, you don't need to put your wine on a diet. But a fat wine does tend to be high in alcohol and fruit, with a strong, bold taste. No shrinking violet here!

Finish. Does the taste of the wine linger even after you've swallowed? The longer the finish, the better the wine.

Flabby. Forget about the little barbells for this wine. Flabby just means the wine is thin, weak, and lacking any acidity. These wines go on our cooking wine shelf or down the drain.

Hot. This gets back to that wine that burned your nose on sniffing; it has way too much alcohol. Be careful with this one. Sometimes, if you let it sit for a while, or decant it, some of the alcohol evaporates.

Oaky. This is a classic wine term. Basically, it means

you're getting a vanilla flavor, a vestige of the oak barrels in which the wine was aged.

Tannic. This is a biggie in the wine-tasting world. Tannins come from the wine skins and seeds, so they are primarily found in red wines. Tannins are the same natural chemicals that make tea bitter. But they also provide structure and backbone to wine, as well as acting as a natural preservative that lets wine age. If a wine is tannic, you'll know it, as your tongue puckers up. This is generally a good wine to decant if you want to drink it now, or else put it away in the cellar for a few years to "soften."

Tight. This is a wine that's wound as tightly as a pro football coach whose team is down by seven with a first down and twenty-five seconds to go in the fourth quarter. Give this wine some time—either in the glass or a decanter—and it will "open up." This is the breathing we referred to earlier in this chapter.

Don't forget the importance of your own language, perhaps with that special someone or your wine friends. For instance, Keith knows just what Debra means when she tastes a wine, pauses, then looks at him and says, "Buy more." You could come up with your own definition for a "sexy" wine.

And don't go overboard. Here's one that made us laugh. The legendary wine writer Alexis Bespaloff (aka André Simon) described a 1905 Margaux in his 1930s book, *Fireside Book of Wine*: "The 1905 was simply delightful; fresh, sweet and charming, a girl of fifteen, who is already a great artist, coming on tiptoes and curtseying herself out with childish grace and laughing blue eyes."

Give us a break. It's just wine!

CHAPTER 3

WINNING WHITE WINES

*F*or many people, white wine is *it*. It just seems so much more accessible, so easy to say, "I'll have a glass of white wine, please." And who can forget the Chablis craze of the 1970s and '80s? (As you'll learn later, you were probably drinking cheap Chardonnay.) In fact, we know several women who refuse to drink anything else, saying red wine gives them a headache.

Hey, we love white wines, too. Not to the exclusion of reds, but certainly nothing is better when you're dining on oysters on the half shell, or a delicate crabmeat ravioli with cream sauce, or just sitting out on the patio on one of those warm summer evenings that never seems to end. And, surprisingly enough, we've even found whites that work well with heavier meat meals and provide a spicy warmth during the worst a northern winter can dish out.

Plus, if you're just getting into wine, the whites are a great place to start. So let's get started!

In this chapter, we focus on the most commonly available types of white wine: Chardonnay, Sauvignon Blanc (aka Fumé Blanc), Pinot Gris (aka Pinot Grigio), Riesling, and the one that gives the wine clerk at our

OF WINE AND HEADACHES

We know lots of people who swear that they can't drink red wine without getting a headache, but do fine with white wine. It's not all in their heads. Studies do support the reality of something called "red wine headache" or RWH. These headaches tend to occur within thirty minutes to three hours of drinking the wine and occur after just a glass or two.

In one seminal study at Bernhard Baron Memorial Research Laboratories at Queen Charlotte's Hospital in London, researchers had eleven people prone to migraines drink either red wine or a diluted vodka mixture (the drinks were disguised in dark bottles so the participants didn't know which was which). Nine of the eleven had a migraine attack after drinking the red wine; none had even a slight headache after imbibing the vodka, leading researchers to speculate that something in the red wine, not alcohol, triggers migraines.

One theory is that high levels of tannins in red wine trigger the pain by increasing levels of the chemical serotonin in the brain. High levels of serotonin can cause headaches, particularly migraines. That theory falls apart, however, when researchers point out that people don't get headaches from tea or dark chocolate—which also have high tannin levels.

wine store the giggles when people try to pronounce it—Gewürztraminer. But these aren't the only whites around. So don't be afraid to try a white varietal or blend you never heard of.

Some people swear it must be the sulfites in wine. Sulfites are preservatives sometimes used in wine to maintain its freshness. About 1 percent of the population is allergic to sulfites. But that allergy triggers breathing problems, not headaches. Plus, sulfite levels are often higher in dry white wines. Some evidence points to substances called histamines, which are much higher in red wine than white wine. Some people can't process histamines in their bodies, and headache is one sign of histamine intolerance.

Regardless of what causes wine-related headaches, what's most important is preventing them. One option is to take an aspirin about an hour before you start drinking; there's some evidence this might help prevent the headache. The other is to take an antihistamine an hour before you start drinking; this can help if you're sensitive to histamines. You may find that only *some* wines provoke headaches; the worst migraine Debra ever had came after a couple of glasses of the house wine at an Italian restaurant. If you find a wine that doesn't hurt your head, stick with it.

Finally, of course, remember our mantra: All things in moderation. No matter what you're drinking, if you overdo it, you *will* get a headache!

USING THE WINE CHAPTERS

To make it easier to keep track of the information we're going to throw at you in this and the following chapters, we've devised an easy-to-use format. The first part of each wine description tells you about the wine itself, where it's grown, what makes it unique. Then comes

Vinicultural Vocabulary: words typically used to describe the wine.

Best With: foods that work best with the wine.

Wines That Just Can't Miss: our suggestions of widely available labels to try in three categories:

- **Everyday wines.** These wines, priced around $15 or less are for, well, everyday drinking. They're what you choose when you don't want to spend a lot but still want a tasty bottle for Tuesday night's baked chicken.
- **Friday night wines.** These wines cost a bit more—up to $40—but provide the extra specialness you want for the end of the workweek, a dinner party with friends, or a "date night."
- **High roller wines.** These wines are for the big spenders. No holds barred on this wine—it's to celebrate your child's graduation from college, to toast your engagement, or to commemorate the new job. These prices can go anywhere from $40 to hundreds of dollars. The sky's the limit!

MAKING WHITE WINE

You can make white wine from red grapes but you cannot make red wine from green grapes. That's because the skin of the grapes gives red wine its color. Thus, most major white wines come from green or pink grapes.

Winemakers use a different process when they make white wine. While the picking and crushing and pressing are the same, instead of allowing the juice to ferment along with the seeds and skins, as with red, the juice ferments on its own. The skins and seeds, by the way, are often spread in the vineyard as fertilizer.

Most wineries also try to keep white wine grapes cool before they're crushed. This prevents oily flavors in the skins from being drawn out. That's also why vineyards transport white wine grapes in refrigerated containers or pick the grapes at night.

Most modern whites are fermented in temperature-controlled steel vats and only see oak in the later stages. Sometimes the oak is oak barrels, sometimes it is pieces of oak thrown into steel fermenters.

It's also quicker to make a white wine than a red wine. Inexpensive white wines are usually bottled within six months of harvest, compared to a couple of years for reds.

Even barrel-aged wines don't spend too much time in oak—six to eighteen months at most.

There are two more words you need to know about the making of white wines: *chaptalization* and *acidification*.

If the grapes don't have quite enough sugar to create the right amount of alcohol, winemakers use chaptalization, which means they add sugar or concentrated grape juice. This technique is used most often when grapes are grown in cool climates. Sure, it's easy enough to add sugar, but some wine-growing/making areas have laws preventing such adulteration.

Acidification is used when the opposite problem exists—too much sugar and not enough acidity. Here, acid is added in the form of malic or citric acid (relatively cheap) or more expensive tartaric acid. This is often done with Chardonnay, the first of the whites on our list.

WINE PIONEER: JESS JACKSON

In California, heck, in the entire United States, Jess Jackson is considered the man who revived Chardonnay. He's also the lawyer who built the wine empire called Kendall Jackson.

It was actually a matter of luck that led to Jackson's winning formula when his 1983 fermentation stopped fermenting before all the sugar turned into alcohol. The result: a hint of sweetness that swept wine lovers (and critics, at least back then) off their feet.

Believe it or not, today's Kendall Jackson Chardonnays have dried out quite a bit and are only half as sweet as those of yore. If you like the low-end, grocery store Vintner's Reserve, save your pennies and try one of Jackson's higher-end Chards, such as his Grand Reserve or Highland Estates wines ($18 to $45).

COMING TO TERMS WITH CHARDONNAY

In a wonderful scene in the beginning of the wine lovers' movie *Sideways*, the main character, wine snob Miles, says to his wine-novice friend, Jack: "I like all varietals. I just don't generally like the way they manipulate Chardonnay in California. Too much oak and secondary malolactic fermentation."

Too much malo-*what?*

The first thing you should know is that Miles (or the screenwriter) was redundant. Secondary fermentation *is* malolactic fermentation—the two are the same. The terms refer to the bacterial change that starts after the initial fermentation. This softens the crispness of the wine and enhances any buttery notes as the sharp-tasting malic acids are transformed into softer, riper-tasting lactic acids.

Some believe, however, that this process may reduce the lifespan of the wine. Others, like our friend Miles, blame it for the homogenization of Chardonnay, as it results in an easier-to-drink, easier-to-like wine.

And yes, it's true that many winemakers use malolactic fermentation to make their Chardonnays appeal to the taste buds of the masses with a sweetish, soft, buttery wine that has obviously spent lots of time in or around oak.

In fact, this is the type of formula that made a fortune for Chardonnay vintner Jess Jackson, owner of the Kendall Jackson winery. His approachable, easy-to-drink and easy-to-like mass-produced Vintner's Reserve Chardonnay, which typically retails for about $12, sells more than 2 million cases a year and is copied by hundreds of other winemakers eager to please American Chard drinkers.

This easy-to-drink formula is also what makes Chardonnay the most popular white wine in the country (chances are, Chardonnay is what you get if you just ask for a glass of white wine at a restaurant or bar) and many wineries rely on their Chards for most of their profits.

But a really *good* Chard should be much more than just creamy and soft. It should also have a strong backbone of fruit and acidity, something you're much more likely to find in a Chardonnay from France, Australia, or New Zealand than one from California.

Having said that, we want to reiterate our primary premise for this book: The best wine is the one *you* like—not what the critics (or wannabe-wine-writers) tell you that you *should* like. For instance, while many sophisticated wine lovers turn their noses down at soft, buttery Chardonnays, Deb (and sometimes Keith) happens to love them.

Some attribute the versatility of Chardonnay to the fact that it is a somewhat neutral grape, making it an ideal canvas for the expression of terroir. And it's true that Chardonnays from cooler climates like New Zealand and France tend to be fruitier, while those from warmer climates (think Australia and California) tend to have more honeyed overtones, sometimes with a roasted flavor breaking through.

When it comes to color, a Chardonnay can cover the full palette from a very pale straw-like color to a robust "scotch-like" hue almost verging on orange. No matter the color, the wine should be clear, not cloudy. A cloudy Chard is a bad Chard, especially if it's young (less than five years). This is an indication that too much air has gotten into the bottled wine, turning it into high-end vinegar.

CHARDONNAY: VINICULTURAL VOCABULARY

People who love wine love to talk about wine. Often, their comments are published in magazines or online. You may often find these "tasting notes" displayed near the wine in stores. Tasting notes for Chardonnays typically include terms like apricot, pineapple, nectarines, pears, apples, toast, buttered toast, and vanilla. Most of these are pretty self-explanatory.

But then tasters start adding terms such as "mineral," leaving you totally lost. Don't be. Take a pebble (preferably a clean one) from a stream or your garden and stick it in your mouth. Roll it around. Memorize the taste. That's mineral.

CHARDONNAY: BEST WITH . . .

Personally, we like Chardonnay as an aperitif, but then again, we like all wines as aperitifs. Traditionally, Chardonnay is paired with "light" foods such as fish and chicken. Some suggest that the oakier versions, however, can stand up to garlicky dips, guacamole, and even Thai coconut dishes.

When Keith was in Australia it was common to have Chardonnays at Christmas. Odd, you might say, but then again remember Christmas in Australia is typically celebrated with a "barbie" poolside! In other words, Chardonnays go really well with barbecued shrimp, burgers, and other grilled meats.

CHARDONNAY: WINES THAT JUST CAN'T MISS

Everyday wines. For an everyday Chardonnay, there are so many choices you may become dizzy even before you start drinking. The Yellow Tail brand from Down Under (Australia) certainly has its followers, and at $7 it's hard to go wrong. It's also hard to find a bad wine from any of the big California brands, including Kendall Jackson, Robert Mondavi, or Gallo. Our main choice, however, is an R. H. Phillips Toasted Head Russian River Valley Chardonnay, running about $15.

Friday night wines. For that end-of-the-week bottle, try a 2005 Au Bon Climat Santa Barbara County Chardonnay (about $30). It's a nice, lighter-style Chardonnay with a balanced blend of fruitiness wrapped in a light vanilla coat.

High roller wines. When the occasion calls for something truly special, yes, you could pick up a bottle of 1995 Domaine de la Romanee Conti Montrachet. Of course, at around $1,000 it may set you back more than you paid for your first car. In our opinion, no wine is worth that much. Instead, stick with high quality California producers such as Peter Michael, Marcassin, and Kistler. These wines still cost a pretty penny—between $75 and $200 or more—but provide far more value for the dollar. If you want to go by the numbers (that is, the wine ratings), try the 2002 Leeuwin Estates Art Series Chardonnay Margaret River, retailing for about $80.

SNAPPY SAUVIGNON BLANC

When we think of Sauvignon Blanc (pronounced *SAH-ven-yawn-blonk*), we think summertime. The wine just smells that way. Crisp and light, it's filled with the aromas of fresh-cut grass, grapefruit, and green apples. Sauvignon

WHENCEFORTH CHABLIS?

Don't bother scouring the wine aisles for the cheap California wine once labeled "Chablis." Chablis is a region of France, but the "Chablis" wines so popular in the late 1970s and early 1980s were really just inferior California Chardonnay. Apparently, some marketing wizard decided that "Chablis" just sounded sexier. But these wines got such a bad reputation for quality, that today the only non-French wine you'll find labeled as "Chablis" is inexpensive jug wine.

Blanc is an everyman (or woman) wine, widely available, relatively cheap, and eminently drinkable.

It hasn't always been this way. Back in the 1970s, Sauvignon Blanc was low on most winemaker and wine drinker lists because of its harsh style. Until, that is, savvy Robert Mondavi (see "Wine Pioneer," page 4), stuck with long-term contracts with growers for the grapes, created a lighter wine, rechristened it Fumé Blanc, and used his marketing expertise to reignite demand.

One problem: He never trademarked the name, which dozens of other winemakers appropriated (don't worry; he's done pretty well, nonetheless).

Sauvignon Blanc also masquerades under other monikers, including Sancerre or Pouilly-Fumé when it's made from the sauvignon blanc grapes of the Loire Valley or Graves region of Bordeaux, both in France.

These days, it's hard to think of Sauvignon Blanc without connecting the name with New Zealand. There is a flood of excellent Sauvignon Blanc coming from that country, where the climate seems to stress the grapes just enough to really bring out their best. New Zealand Sauvignon Blanc tends to be full of acids, extremely crisp, and somewhat steely. Those from California have a more citrusy appeal, often with a hint of oak, while a French Sancerre brings a bit of grapefruit laced with lemon to the glass.

That's because different vintners take different approaches to the fermentation of this wine. In the Loire Valley in France, fermentation occurs in either wood or steel tanks at fairly high temperatures. This avoids the tropical fruit emphasis seen in the cooler fermented New Zealand wines, while reflecting the French desire to create wines that reflect the terroir rather than the grape.

To get the frequently elusive balance between sugar ripeness, acidity, aroma, and fruit that a good Sauvignon Blanc demands, the right climate is essential. The sauvignon blanc grape is a late budder and early ripener that doesn't like too much heat. If it gets overly warm, you might end up with slightly vegetal taste/smell (think cabbage), which, believe it or not, some people actually like—but which we don't!

SAUVIGNON BLANC: VINICULTURAL VOCABULARY
Tasting notes for Sauvignon Blanc wines often use terms such as tart, crisp, tangy, zesty, citrusy, and grassy. These describe the relatively high levels of acidity in the wine compared to the fruitiness.

Various fruits such as limes, pineapple, nectarines, grapefruit, guava, passion fruit, and green apples also turn up in tasting notes, as well as a few unexpected plants and vegetables, including fresh-cut grass, sweet peas, asparagus, and bell peppers. You may even see various mineral terms used, such as flint, steely, and talcum powder.

SAUVIGNON BLANC: BEST WITH . . .

Sauvignon Blanc typically has enough acidity to stand up to spicy food such as peppered tuna, Thai dishes, Szechuan Chinese, and even Mexican (though it's often safer to just stick to beer). Sauvignon Blanc is also ideal as an aperitif on hot summer days. Sauvignon would also be our choice for pasta and clam sauce, simple tortellini dishes, or baked cod or other white fish.

In Chapter 7, you'll read about sauternes, a dessert wine made with sauvignon blanc grapes that is to die for.

SAUVIGNON BLANC: WINES THAT JUST CAN'T MISS

Everyday wines. Pretty much any Sauvignon Blanc from New Zealand or South Africa will go over well. The Nobilo Sauvignon Blanc Marlborough sells for about $8 and the Boschendal Sauvignon Blanc Grand Cuvée about $16. If you want a U.S. variety that's a bit creamier, try one of our favorites: Hogue Cellars Fumé Blanc (usually available for under $12) from Washington State.

Friday night wines. Even for higher-end Sauvignons we head to New Zealand. Try a Cloudy Bay Sauvignon Blanc, an iconoclastic wine that really put New Zealand on the wine map in 1985. The 2006 sells for about $30.

High roller wines. When the menu sports lobster and the occasion calls for something special, we recommend Robert Mondavi's Fumé Blanc To-Kalon Estate, $35 to $70 a bottle, depending on vintage and availability.

PICKING UP ON PINOT GRIGIO (PINOT GRIS)

When we see any Pinot Grigio (*PEE-noh-gree-jeo*), we immediately think of Italy, where this Pinot offshoot is grown. Speculation is that it was brought to Italy from France by medieval monks. Today it's the number one imported Italian varietal in the United States.

But the United States has its own version of this white wine, with Oregon taking the lead for some outstanding Pinot Gris (as it's called in this country). It's no wonder; the pinot gris (pronounced *PEE-no gree*) grape is a direct mutation of the pinot noir grape, for which Oregon is also famous (more on Pinot Noir in Chapter 4). By the way, *gris* means "gray." But why you'd burden a richly flavored wine like Pinot Gris with the bland moniker of "gray" is beyond us. And, in case you were wondering, *pinot* means "pinecone," an apt name since all pinot grapes grow in pinecone-shaped bunches.

In addition to Italy and Oregon (and some parts of California), Pinot Gris also hails from Germany, where it's a Rubenesque wine called either Grauburgunder (dry) or Ruländer (sweet); and the Alsace region of France, where it's called Tokay d'Alsace.

This is the wine you drink if you like Chardonnay but want to set yourself apart. It's stronger than Sauvignon Blanc (in taste, not alcohol), enabling it to stand up to heartier food. It's also got more of the creaminess many like in Chardonnay, a type of richness that's often missing in other whites.

Nonetheless, like Sauvignon Blanc, Pinot Grigio is an ideal wine for hot summer days (and nights). It's also gaining great strides in popularity, bypassing Sauvignon Blanc to become the second most popular white wine sold in the United States.

PINOT GRIGIO: VINICULTURAL VOCABULARY

Pinot Grigio is a light-to-medium bodied wine with mellow flavors, often with a predominantly apricot aroma/taste. Tasting notes used to describe Pinot Grigio include the words spicy, musky, and honeyed.

While Italian Pinot Grigio tends to be a simple, light, crisp wine, those from Oregon have more pear and spice cake flavors. California Pinot Gris, on the other hand, can span the gamut from light and crisp to creamy with overtones of apple.

PINOT GRIGIO: BEST WITH . . .

Try this versatile white with pastas with creamy white sauces, pesto, seafood ravioli, and white meats such as pork, veal, and poultry. Pinot Grigio is similar to Sauvignon Blanc when it comes to food pairings, thanks to its innate sharpness, or acidity, which lets it cut through creamy foods. While a buttery Chardonnay would disappear behind the softness of a fettuccini Alfredo, these whites show nicely.

PINOT GRIGIO: WINES THAT JUST CAN'T MISS

Everyday wines. Stick to any Pinot Grigio from Italy and you'll do great. One getting a lot of favorable mentions is Kupelwieser's Pinot Grigio Alt Adige, retailing for about $13.

Friday night wines. Our top pick: Sokol Blosser, again from Oregon. The 2006 Pinot Gris Dundee Hills Cuvée sells for about $20 and has an interesting blend of peppery almond to counterbalance its apple and orange peel fruitiness.

High roller wines. With a bit more to spend, head to France (or the French section of your local wine store) for a bottle of Zind-Humbrecht Pinot Gris Clos Windsbuh (2004), about $60. This is a great investment given the wine's beautiful blend of smoky apricot and marmalade, coupled with a nice long finish.

THE REALITY OF RIESLING

Wine Spectator publisher Marven Shanken suggests that riesling may be the world's most underappreciated white grape. It should only take one sip of this clean, crisp wine to convince you he's right.

Originating in the steep hillsides of Germany's Mosel and Rhine rivers, the riesling grape thrives on

the sun exposure it receives in those precipitous vineyards. Now widely planted in cool areas around the
world including Russia (when was the last time you
had a Russian wine?), New Zealand, and the United
States (particularly New York and Washington states),
Riesling (pronounced *REE-zling*) is leaving its Teutonic
roots behind.

Still, Germany remains home to the greatest con-
centration of riesling grapes, with some 50,000 acres
planted with the varietal, followed by Australia and
France's Alsace region.

Rieslings are among the few white wines that benefit from aging. In their youth, they are defined by their
fruitiness. As they reach middle age, they take on more
honeyed tones as their fruitiness matures into a candied
taste. This provides a fuller mouthfeel with lanolin or
beeswax notes. Some top-quality Rieslings from producers such as Schloss Schönborn and Dr. Loosen can
age for twenty-five to fifty years, while late harvest versions (covered in Chapter 7) can be cellared for more
than a century.

The reputation of Rieslings was somewhat marred
by the success of Liebfraumilch (Blue Nun) and other
sweet plonk in the late '70s and early '80s. These wines
became very popular because they were sweet and easy
to drink, almost like soda pop, but they were so one-
dimensional in their overwhelming sweetness that people
who appreciate wine for its variety and uniqueness turned
against all Rieslings. This was unfair to many good
Rieslings that offer more challenging notes and tastes.

Today, drier versions from good German producers and the Alsace region of France dominate. These

wines are often low in alcohol, relatively light bodied but with a nice balance between slight sweetness and crisp acidity. To make sure you're getting the drier version, look for the word *kabinett*—the lightest and driest of any German wine. Want something a bit sweeter? *Spätlese* or *auslese* will get you there.

For a special treat, pick up a German Riesling from the 2003 vintage. A massive heat wave in Europe that summer created wines that wine reviewer Ronn Wiegand called the "ripest and richest ever produced."

RIESLING: VINICULTURAL VOCABULARY

Tasting notes for Rieslings use adjectives such as aromatic, vibrant, and juicy. We also see "a sweet mouthful of honey toast," dried peach flavors, and, strangely enough, fresh mushrooms. Other flavors include pineapple, orange marmalade, honey, clove, mineral, and green apple.

Here's how one reviewer describes a Riesling: "A hint of sweetness offsets that lemon, green apple, quince, and mineral flavors." What we want to know is how many people have ever actually tasted (or smelled) a quince?

RIESLING: BEST WITH . . .

The combination of fresh fruit and mouthwatering acidity, combined with the lack of oaky flavors, makes Riesling a great match for a wide variety of cuisines. Try it with noodle or pasta-based salads, shrimp cocktail, cold cracked crab, or steamed clams. And don't be afraid to try it with spicy food such as Thai or Indian. Also white fish, salmon, and even pork and chicken (to be honest, though, what *doesn't* go with chicken?) work well with these wines.

RIESLING: WINES THAT JUST CAN'T MISS

Everyday wines. Stick to a Riesling from Australia, which tends to offer the best values. We suggest a Rosemount Estate Diamond Label Riesling, which you should be able to find for about $10.

Friday night wines. Now it's time to move to another continent and try a Riesling from Germany's Mosel-Saar-Ruwer or Rheingau regions. Dr. Loosen Erdener Pralat Auslese is a consistent winner at about $25. If you want to stay in the United States, try the Château St. Michelle Eroica Riesling from Washington State, about $18: a blend of classic mineral notes with an overtone of rich peach.

High roller wines. If we had to pick one, we'd go for the 2000 Trimbach Cuvée Frederic Emile Riesling from Alsace ($42), rated the number one wine for 2005 by *Wine Enthusiast* magazine. For you big high rollers, a bottle of Zind-Humbrecht, about $70, is again a great choice. The 2001 Domaine Zind-Humbrecht Riesling Brand is described by Pierre Rovani in the October 2003 issue of the *Wine Advocate* as "one of the greatest dry Rieslings I have ever tasted." Kind of hard to ignore that level of praise!

GET SOME GEWÜRZTRAMINER

So it's darn hard to pronounce (*ghe-VERTS-tru-meen-er*). But this wine is well worth the effort. Full-bodied with floral and peppery notes, Gewürztraminer is strong enough to stand up to heavy, hearty German fare, yet light enough for floating in the pool on a summer evening. Although most are produced in the Alsace region of France, you can find some from American winemakers. These, however, are usually sweeter than the dry French or German versions. That doesn't mean they're not luscious, just that they're different from what you may have been used to.

These wines tend to age well and, as you'll see in Chapter 7, they make great dessert wines.

GEWÜRZTRAMINER: VINICULTURAL VOCABULARY

When people describe Gewürztraminer wine they use all sorts of terms to try to pin down the scent and spiciness of this never-dull elixir. One example penned by esteemed wine writer Oz Clarke in *Oz Clarke's Encyclopedia of Grapes* goes like this: "You get a grape that combines a most irresistible scent of lychees and tea rose petals with the lushness of tropical fruit, the bite of black pepper, and the intimate dressing room aroma of Nivea cream . . ." We're okay with the rose petals and tropical fruit, even the bite of black pepper, but the "intimate dressing room aroma of Nivea cream" just has to go.

More commonly used descriptors for Gewürztraminer include fruity, peppery, "filled with flowers," bracing, citrusy, good acids, spice, and musk.

And, in case you were wondering, a lychee (often seen in wine descriptions) is a rare subtropical fruit from China, where it's called "King of Fruits." The oval or heart-shaped fruit is about two inches long, with red, bumpy skin. The crisp juicy flesh tastes somewhat sweeter than a grape, with high levels of acid and freshness. Thus, it's perfect for white wine descriptions.

GEWÜRZTRAMINER: BEST WITH . . .

Excellent by itself as an aperitif, Gewürztraminer has enough acidity and balance to stand up to heavy meats such as pork, foods with cream sauces, and spicy cuisines such as Indian, Chinese, and Asian fusion. Gewürztraminer is also a good choice with crackers and cheese at the start of a dinner party, and an excellent option for foie gras if you don't have any Sauternes handy (more on Sauternes in Chapter 7).

GEWÜRZTRAMINER: WINES THAT JUST CAN'T MISS

Everyday wines. Although the California Gewürztraminers are somewhat sweeter than the Alsatian, we recommend a Château St. Jean Sonoma County Gewürztraminer, which you should be able to find for $12, or an Adler Fels, Sonoma County, which retails for about $15.

Friday night wines. One small step up in complexity and price gets you to the Domaine Trimbach Gewürztraminer, retailing for about $20. With notes of spice, green apple, plum, and nutmeg, it represents all that is good about this unique varietal.

High roller wines. Try the Gewürztraminer Turckheim from Domaine Zind-Humbrecht, about $40. Tasting notes call it "an intensely flavored, powerful Gewürztraminer, featuring a complex array of aromas and flavors—grapefruit, orange, lychee, honey, smoke and spice . . ."

DON'T FORGET THESE WHITES

Obviously, we didn't cover every white wine out there. Some you'll learn about in Chapter 7 on dessert wines. But the following three are also worth searching for, although they won't be as easily found as the varietals already discussed.

Viognier. Think of angels, honey, and flowers, and you will understand the appeal of Viognier. This varietal is rooted in France and is just gaining ground in the United States. It's a great alternative to overoaked Chardonnays, with more character than Pinot Grigio. But don't bother aging it; this is a wine meant to be chilled and drunk today.

Chenin Blanc. If you thought Chardonnay was the top export from France, think again. It's actually a grape called chenin blanc, and during the 1970s it was as popular in this country as bell-bottoms and leisure suits. These days, it goes by several aliases, depending on where it hails from. In Central and South America it's called Pinot Blanco; in South Africa, it's Steen; in its native France it's known as Pineau de la Loire; and in the United States you may see it called Vouvray. It's still very popular (it's the third most grown white wine grape in California), not surprising given its dry, light mineral taste that works great with food. Like Viognier, it's meant to be drunk young.

Semillon. We're not going to say much about this grape here because you'll read more about it in the dessert wine chapter. Suffice it to say that the semillon grape is at the heart of the greatest sweet wine of all: Château d'Yquem. However, we're seeing Semillon appear more often on store shelves, blended with Sauvignon Blanc and on its own. Look for Semillon from Chile, which grows more of this grape varietal than any other country.

CHAPTER 4

HEAVY HITTER REDS

*W*hen we first approached this chapter, we planned to cover all red wines in just one chapter. Then we realized that it would be a very *looooonnnng* chapter. There are just *so many* red wines.

So to make it easier on you (and us) we broke it in two. This chapter highlights the top five red varietals: Cabernet Sauvignon, Merlot, Pinot Noir, Syrah (or Shiraz), and Zinfandel, and in Chapter 5 we try to cover much of the remainder.

As you learned in Chapter 3, while you can make white wines from red grapes, you cannot make red wines from green grapes. That's because the skin of the grape gives the wine its color. The longer the contact with the skin, the stronger the color. Thus you can find reds ranging from rosy Beaujolais to inky black Zinfandels.

The skins contribute more than just color, however; they're also the main source of tannins (along with the stems and seeds). We talked a bit about tannins in Chapter 2, but it's worth repeating.

Tannins, or that slightly bitter taste you get from some wines that makes your mouth pucker, are one of

the main components that give red wines their structure, or backbone. The others are acids, alcohol, fruit,
and glycerol (a sugar alcohol). Some varietals have lots
of tannins (Cabernet Sauvignon), some only moderate
amounts (Pinot Noir). The more tannins in a wine, the
longer it can age. With age, the tannins soften but don't
disappear, leaving a more complex wine in their path.

Now, onto the meat, uh, wine, of the chapter.

MAGNIFICENT MERLOT

Merlot is the Rodney Dangerfield of red wines; it just
can't get any respect. This is especially true after the
bashing it took in the aforementioned movie *Sideways*,
in which the main character trashed Merlot. After that
movie came out, sales of Merlot plummeted. But the
movie was just giving voice to what many already knew:
After Merlot first rose to popularity in the 1980s, too
many wine producers began making too much overly
fruity, insipid Merlot that all tasted the same.

Merlot is a noble grape, one of the two primary
grapes in Bordeaux wines. The Bordeaux region of
France boasts more Merlot vines than anywhere else in
the world. You might say that Cabernet Sauvignon and
Merlot are the perfect couple, with Merlot's softness
blurring the high tannins of Cabernet. In fact, while in
Sideways Miles trashes Merlot, his most precious bottle
of wine is a 1961 Château Cheval Blanc: a blend of
Merlot and Cabernet!

Merlot's softness and inherent drinkability is the
reason it's sometimes described as a beginner's red

wine. It's also an easy-to-understand wine, one that needs little aging and is usually ready to drink just as soon as you can uncork it.

Unfortunately, too much of the low-priced Merlot on the market today tastes all the same—like alcoholic fruit juice. Once you pass the $20 price range, however, you'll find Merlots with much more complexity and uniqueness, wines that have their own individuality instead of tasting like some fast-food homogenous version of wine.

MERLOT: VINICULTURAL VOCABULARY

Tasting notes for Merlot are often sprinkled with words such as black cherry and plums, chocolate, fruit cake, and vanilla. Other fruit tastes that come out in this wine include strawberries, raspberries, black currants, damson plums, figs, and prunes. Good Merlot also has a spiciness—typically cinnamon and cloves, but occasionally sandalwood. You may also taste truffles, tobacco, licorice, and toasted nuts. And if you luck out with a truly fine bottle, you'll also get notes of chocolate, mocha, and coffee.

MERLOT: BEST WITH . . .

Merlots are soft, fruity wines that work well with and without food. They're traditionally paired with gamey foods such as pheasant, duck, and goose. However, bolder versions can stand up to subtly spiced curries and even Indian tandoori dishes, although really spicy foods might overwhelm the wine.

Frankly, we love ours with grilled hamburgers eaten outside on warm summer evenings!

MERLOT: WINES THAT JUST CAN'T MISS

Everyday wines. Unfortunately, everyday Merlot lovers may have to kiss quite a few frogs before finding their prince. There's an awful lot of cheap, mediocre Merlot out there that's sweet, syrupy, and boring. Look hard enough, however, and the gems appear. Columbia Crest Winery Merlot Two Vines is a steal at $7, as is Rosemount Estate's Merlot Diamond label, also about $7. Other choices: Camelot's Merlot California, rich with vanilla, cherry, and a hint of brambly spice for about $10, or the Yalumba Merlot Y series for about $11.

Friday night wines. You can't go wrong with any vintage of Ehlers Estate Merlot, a small winery we discovered in the northern end of the Napa Valley. For a Friday evening or weekend wine we highly recommend Ehlers Estate 2005 St. Helena Merlot, about $45 to $50. If you can't find it in your local wine store, contact the winery: www.ehlersestate.com. Or try Provenance Vineyards Merlot Napa Valley, complete with complex flavors of currants and pencil lead (a good thing, believe us), and about $30 for the 2004 vintage. Or try the 2001 St. Francis Behler Vineyard Reserve Merlot, about $30.

High roller wines. The pinnacle of Merlot is the Bordeaux wine Château Petrus, from the winery of the same name, and is 95 percent Merlot and 5 percent Cabernet. Wine writers describe it as the region's "most intensely concentrated, richly flavored, and unique red wine," and "nothing more than one of the most satisfying, most profound wines that tastes as good at the end of the bottle as at the beginning." It has a price tag to match. Depending on the year, be prepared to pay upward of $1,000. We

WINE PIONEER: EHLERS ESTATE

From the outside, Ehlers Estate in St. Helena, California, resembles any other small, independent winery along the Silverado Trail. The requisite stone gates. The long drive leading up to the rustic tasting/barrel/administrative building. The barking collie with the run of the vineyards.

On the back end, however, Ehlers is significantly different from any other boutique winery in Napa or, for that matter, most of the world. Ehlers Estate is owned by a nonprofit, Paris-based foundation. So rather than paying off debt, satisfying stockholders, or banking a nest egg for an absentee dot-com millionaire, a percentage of its sales go to the Leducq Foundation, a philanthropic entity devoted to, appropriately enough, international cardiovascular research. Ehlers is the only winery in the world (that we know of) to support medical research.

saw a 2003 priced at $2,400 (yes, per bottle!). If your pockets aren't *quite* that deep, go for a 2004 Pahlmeyer Merlot, from the California winery of the same name, which retails for about $90, or a Hartwell Merlot Stags Leap District 2003, for about $75.

CABERNET SAUVIGNON: THE KING OF REDS

If there is a universal red wine grape, it has to be cabernet sauvignon. Google it and you get more than 3.2 million hits. By itself, the grape tends to produce big, tannic wines that often need years of aging to mellow. Many high-end California Cabernets tend to epitomize this description, producing hugely powerful Cabernets that command huge prices.

Some of these wines have come to be known as "cult" Cabernets because they're produced in small amounts and sold only through the winery to those who are lucky enough to get on the mailing list.

And they're pricey. Thirty bottles of the cult wine Screaming Eagle (three from each vintage from 1992 to 2002) sold at auction in 2006 for $47,970—about $1,600 a bottle. Put another way, one teaspoon of that wine cost about $10. And that's for a wine that typically overpowers any food it's drunk with, and for which you have no guarantee of quality as you won't even open it for years.

That's why, for a great Cabernet at a great value, we steer toward Australia. With constant sunshine, warm temperatures, and no risk of late frosts to damage the fruit just before harvest, Australian Cabernets offer a consistently good product at an affordable price. While you'll find tannins in these and other less expensive Cabernets, that doesn't mean they have to age. Most Cabernets on the market today have just enough tannin to provide a good backbone, not so much that you need to stick them in a cellar to soften for ten years.

CABERNET SAUVIGNON: VINICULTURAL VOCABULARY

Typical descriptors of a quality Cabernet include black currant, black cherries, cigar box, pencil shavings, creosote, tar, and bell pepper. Cabernet is a dry wine (meaning less sugar) and is considered a medium- or full-bodied wine, which means it pairs well with strongly flavored foods.

CABERNET SAUVIGNON: BEST WITH . . .

It has to be steak! There can be few more heavenly pairings than a thick, aged prime rib and a Cabernet in its prime. Not into red meat? Throw some Portobello mushrooms on the grill basted with a bit of balsamic vinegar and pair that with your Cab. Alternatively, we like our Cab with roasted salmon or blackened tuna or, for dessert, with a piece of dark chocolate or cheddar cheese.

CABERNET SAUVIGNON: WINES THAT JUST CAN'T MISS

Everyday wines. It's nearly impossible to find a good California Cabernet for less than $20. So we recommend you head down under to Australia and go with a Jacob's Creek Reserve Cabernet Sauvignon, less than $15, or a Rosemount Estate Hill of Gold Mudgee, also about $15. For something different, try a Spanish Cabernet. Viñas del Vero's Cabernet Sauvignon Somontano Colección Los Sasos, typically sells for about $15.

Friday night wines. For a bit of a treat, try a Bordeaux. While not 100 percent Cabernet, it does rely on the grape for much of its structure. A couple to look for: Château Malescot-St.-Exupéry's 2002 Margaux (about $20) and Château Beau-Séjour Bécot's 2002 St.-Emilion (about $40).

High roller wines. No question here: the top-rated wine for 2005, the 2002 Joseph Phelps Insignia, about $150. If that's too pricey, check out d'Arenberg's McLaren Vale The Coppermine Road 2002 Cabernet Sauvignon from Australia (about $65) or, if you can find it, Showket's

2002 Oakville Cabernet Sauvignon (about $75). Another great find hails from Jericho Canyon Vineyard, which offers a beautifully rich 2004 Cabernet for about $75.

YOU SAY SYRAH, I SAY SHIRAZ

Syrah (as it's called in France) or Shiraz (as it's called in Australia and the United States) has its roots in France, but it is the quintessential transplant. Introduced into Australia by a Scotsman in 1824, it has put that country's wines on the global map.

Why? Syrah today is where Merlot was ten years ago. It's highly drinkable, very affordable, needs no aging, and goes with almost any kind of food. It's a fruit-forward style wine, meaning it really tastes like fruit, instead of the inside of an oak barrel, but still has enough pepperiness to keep you on your toes. It's also easy to grow anywhere from hillsides to flatlands, and in cool, warm, or hot climates.

SYRAH: VINICULTURAL VOCABULARY
Syrah is a densely flavored wine with thick blackberry and red fruit flavors. You might also note an aroma of violets. Syrah often has a slightly sweet taste due to its dense package of fruit flavors as well as long contact with new oak barrels.

But Syrah is no wimpy wine. The better the Syrah, the stronger the flavors, with terms such as black pepper, leather, or truffles in tasting notes, and even beef jerky, chocolate, and smokiness used to describe its taste.

SYRAH: BEST WITH . . .

Given that these wines are almost always strongly flavored, they naturally pair well with stews, roasted
meats, and heavy red sauces. One favorite pairing is
with cassoulet, a wonderful country French dish that
combines pork, duck, beans, and other hearty foods
into one meltingly succulent stew.

But really, we drink Syrah year-round with nearly
everything except a delicate white fish (which we don't
eat too much of, anyway). Experiment!

SYRAH: WINES THAT JUST CAN'T MISS

Everyday wines. For everyday drinking wines, there's only
one possible choice—our personal favorite: Bin 555 from
Wyndam Estates, any year. You can find it for between $7
and $10; it's a great value. Other good values include any
Syrah from the Hardy's or Rosemount vineyards in
Australia. For a good value U.S. Syrah, try one from the
Covey Run Winery in Washington State, about $10.

Friday night wines. If you're willing to spend a bit more,
pick up Arrowood's 2000 Syrah Sara Lee's Vineyard
from the Russian River Valley in California, about $30.
Other options include Red Willow Syrah from
Columbia Winery in Washington State (about $40) or,
from across the pond (and not forgetting that France is
also a mainstay of the grape), a Guigal Brune et Blonde
Côte-Rôtie (about $60).

High roller wines. For that very special occasion it has to
be a Penfolds Grange, the "first-growth" wine of Australia.
Expect to spend $250 to $300 a bottle depending on

the vintage. Of course, you don't have to lay out that much for a special Syrah. Look for other special Aussie Shirazes, including a Barossa Valley Estate Shiraz Barossa Valley E&E Black Pepper 2002 (about $85) or Elderton's Shiraz Barossa Command 2001 (about $75).

PASSIONATE PINOT NOIR

If Merlots are the Rodney Dangerfield of wines, then Pinots are the Sarah Bernhardt—one of the most emotional wines out there. The grape itself is thin-skinned, with a well-deserved reputation for being among the most challenging to grow.

Yet every winemaker worth his or her yeast seems irresistibly drawn to this grape, propelled by some inner urge to show just what a great wine he or she can produce. And it's true that in the hands of the right artist, this grape becomes a stellar example of modern alchemy in which simple juice becomes an oenophile's version of gold. Domaine de la Romanée-Conti, for example, is a pure Pinot Noir wine that can reach more than $5,000 a bottle.

However, while this grape can result in greatness, it can also create some of the worst-tasting wine ever. As Deb likes to point out: "If you've tasted one Pinot Noir, you've tasted one Pinot Noir." Pinot Noir can be as wimpy as the quintessential 98-pound weakling or as strong as a 300-pound gorilla. The best way to find your favorite? Taste, taste, taste—and then taste again.

We recently opened three Pinot Noir wines from New Zealand's Marlborough region: a 2005 Kim

Crawford, a 2003 Koura Bay, and a 2003 Nobilo Icon. We wanted to taste them at the same time to compare them against one another.

We found all were well-made wines with classical Pinot Noir features: bright color; floral, fruity nose; and nice long finish. We agreed we'd drink any of them again. Then we checked the prices: The Kim Crawford was $11.99, the Nobilo Icon $15.99, and the Koura Bay $27.99. All of which begs the question "If they all taste pretty much the same, why pay twice as much for the Koura Bay as for the Kim Crawford?"

You shouldn't. If you've done your homework, tried a few wines, and decided you prefer the less expensive one (for the taste, not just the price), give yourself a pat on the back and save a few bucks by sticking with the one you like.

The reality is that there really is no rhyme or reason when it comes to wine pricing. We've talked to winery owners who were told to *increase* the price of their wine because it would be taken more seriously. We've tasted $10 bottles that made us close our eyes in ecstasy, and $50 bottles that would have been banished to the cooking wine shelf if it wasn't for the fact that we spent (wasted) $50 on them! Let your nose and mouth lead you when it comes to choosing wine, not your pocketbook.

PINOT NOIR: VINICULTURAL VOCABULARY

Tasting notes for Pinot Noirs tend to get rather flowery. Simple fruit-first Pinots are often described as tasting of strawberries or black cherries, sometimes even Jolly Rancher candies. More complex Pinots have fruitiness, of course, but also some smokiness and earthiness. The easiest way to tell the good stuff from the plonk is in the length of the finish. If you're still tasting the wine twenty to thirty seconds after you swallowed, you've hit a winner.

PINOT NOIR: WINES THAT JUST CAN'T MISS

Everyday wines. Stick with our favorite from our blind tasting: the Kim Crawford. At $16.99 a bottle, this relatively simple yet fruity Pinot is a great choice for any night of the week and its lighter taste makes it perfect with any type of food. Other good values also from California: Castle Rock's Pinot Noir Napa Valley (about $11) and Meridian's Pinot Noir Santa Barbara County (also $11).

Friday night wines. Our vote goes to California's Carneros region in Napa, where we've found a Robert Mondavi Winery Pinot Noir Reserve that retails for about $45. Other ideal ways to end the week include a Keller Estate La Cruz Vineyard Pinot Noir 2005, about $40, or a Mount Eden Pinot Noir Estate Santa Cruz Mountains 2003, about $35.

High roller wines. The real high rollers will gravitate to the classics of Burgundy—and they'll have deep pockets. Too deep for us, to be honest, so we wouldn't even try to advise on what to buy. A more modest but still hedonistic purchase is one of the high end American Pinots, such as the 2004 Williams Selyem Winery Pinot Noir Central Coast, which retails for about $60. This wine packs a concentrated wallop of cherry fruit followed by strawberry cream wrapped in a light but satisfying mouthfeel. Quite a bit more expensive, but worth it in some people's eyes, is the Marcassin Pinot Noir Sonoma Coast Marcassin Vineyard 2001, which retails for about $250.

ZINFANDEL: FORGET THE PINK STUFF

Zinfandel used to be considered California's home-grown success. Until, that is, a professor at the University of California–Davis (which has one of the top wine-related programs in the country) used DNA analysis to trace its roots back to the Dalmatian coast in Croatia. That forced California legislators to change a bill that declared Zinfandel the state wine to one calling it the official "historic" wine.

We're actually lucky that Zinfandel—true, rich, deep, powerful red Zinfandel—has survived in this country. The wine we adore was almost killed in the late 1980s and '90s when a flood of pink Zin hit the shelves. So-called "white Zinfandel" was a huge hit with people who had never drunk wine before but who liked the light, slightly sweet (we'd say too sweet) taste, particularly that made by Sutter Home winery.

Thankfully, the days of pink Zin have waned, if not disappeared entirely. Today, three major wineries dominate the red Zinfandel world in the United States: Ridge, Ravenswood, and Rosenblum. That's why it's hard to go wrong buying a Zinfandel that starts with an "R."

It's a tough call on whether you should age Zins. Personally, we like to drink ours as soon as they're in the house, and if you like really fruity Zins, with gobs of fruit and jamminess, you shouldn't age them. They'll almost certainly lose their freshness within two to four years. On the other hand, Zins with enough tannins to balance the fruitiness may benefit from a few more birthdays.

When buying Zins, check the alcohol content. The grape concentrates so much sugar that some wines end up with an alcohol content of 15 percent and above, making them difficult to match with food and making them more like Port.

ZINFANDEL: VINICULTURAL VOCABULARY

Zins are typically described as big, full-bodied wines tasting of black currants, raspberries, strawberries, plums, prunes, and sometimes raisins (for the really ripe ones). Unripe Zins can sometimes have a very pronounced vegetable taste (not good!) and some occasionally have hints of mint or eucalyptus (good!).

ZINFANDEL: BEST WITH . . .

At the risk of sounding like a broken record, Zins, like many reds, can stand up to pretty much everything from rich stews to roasted turkeys and fine cuts of beef. A personal favorite is Zinfandel paired with Keith's award-winning chili (mild to moderate heat and a bottle or two of Guinness in the sauce). The pairing works because of the slightly sweet edge many Zins have, which nicely balances the chili's spiciness.

ZINFANDEL: WINES THAT JUST CAN'T MISS

Everyday wines. If you can still find it, try the 2003 Buehler Vineyards Napa Valley Zinfandel, which snagged a 93-point score from *Wine Spectator* and costs only about $15 a bottle. Now that's good value! The 2006 is more widely available and still good value at about $20 per bottle. Other everyday drinking Zins include Castle Rock Russian River Valley Zinfandel (about $18) and Rosenblum's Contra Costa County Oakley Vineyards Zinfandel (also about $18).

Friday night wines. We recommend anything from Rosenblum, Ridge, or Ravenswood, particularly the Rosenblum Cellars 2005 Rockpile Vineyard Zinfandel, about $30. Other options: Navarro's 2005 Mendocino Zinfandel (about $20) or the Ridge Zinfandel Paso Robles Dusi Ranch (2005), rich with berry and plum flavors and retailing for around $25.

Heavy roller wines. For that special occasion Zin, go for one from the queen winemaker of Zins: Helen Turley. The 2005 Turley Wine Cellars Howell Mountain Dragon Vineyard Zinfandel (quite a mouthful there) is not only very special but, at $55, not outrageously expensive. Tasting notes for this wine include descriptions of pepper and tobacco aromas preceding dark berry flavors wrapped around robust acidity and enough tannins to ensure a relatively long life. Another one to try comes from Martinelli: the 2002 Russian River Valley Jackass Vineyard Zinfandel, about $170, described as chewy, intense, and rustic.

WHAT'S A HOUSE WINE?

In restaurants, house wine is the wine served by the glass, often cheap and easily forgotten. For us, it's the Bin 555 from Wyndam Estates mentioned earlier, a wine that is inexpensive yet very drinkable and always interesting. It's what we open on a weeknight when we want the comfortable and familiar, or during a dinner party to surprise our guests (they invariably think it's much more expensive than it is). For you, it's the inexpensive wine find that makes the wine uniquely yours!

CHAPTER 5

THE *OTHER* REDS

*W*e call the red wines discussed in this chapter the *other* reds. That's not to imply in any way that these wines are in some way inferior to the classic reds discussed in Chapter 4, only that these are somewhat less common or less available. Some, such as Barolo and Barbaresco, have been around for decades and are less common because they're fairly expensive. Others, such as Malbec and Cabernet Franc, are just escaping their old reputations as blending wines only good for toning down the tannins of Cabernet Sauvignon. (For the record, a blending wine is a wine used in small quantities to smooth the flavor of classic wines such as Bordeaux or Burgundy.)

Unfortunately, we can only hit the highlights here; if we tried to cover every other red wine out there we'd be writing an entire book on just red wine! A conservative estimate is that there are about forty well-known red-wine grapes. So we've focused on those you should know about to know just enough, and given you just a sentence or two on others we think are key.

Okay, to be honest, we've highlighted our favorites.

You can agree or disagree but, after all, *we* are the writers here!

CABERNET FRANC: THE *OTHER* CABERNET

There's a reason Cabernet Franc shares part of a name with Cabernet Sauvignon: It's a parent of the famous varietal. Typically used as a blending grape in wines such as Bordeaux (some years, it makes up 60 percent of the grapes used in the first-growth wine called Cheval-Blanc), it's beginning to come into its own.

While Cabernet Franc is similar to Cabernet Sauvignon, it's less tannic and ready to drink earlier—one reason vintners and wine drinkers have discovered it as a varietal worth taking seriously on its own.

Primarily grown in France and Italy, Cabernet Franc is also popping up in Australia, Chile, and California. Given that it requires fewer days of sun to reach a reasonable level of ripeness, it's turning out to be particularly ideal in cooler-climate wine-growing states such as New York, Virginia, and Washington. In fact, it currently makes up about 10 percent of the grapes grown in Washington State, which makes some of the best Cab Francs on the market.

CABERNET FRANC: VINICULTURAL VOCABULARY

Taste a Cabernet Franc and you'll get strong notes of black currant, plum, and black cherry offset with cedar and spice. You're still likely to find it blended with *some* Cabernet Sauvignon and/or Merlot, but don't worry, the cab franc grape still dominates.

CABERNET FRANC: BEST WITH ...

Anything you'd drink a Cabernet Sauvignon with. To us, that means just about any type of food. But pair Cab Franc with red meats or roasted chicken, maybe with a side of roasted potatoes, for a real taste sensation.

CABERNET FRANC: WINES THAT JUST CAN'T MISS

Everyday wines. For the everyday wine, we recommend an Ironstone Vineyards Cabernet Franc, any year, which retails for about $16. A well-balanced, medium-bodied wine, it has a fresh berry nose and hints of violets, toasted oak, and tobacco.

Friday night wines. It's the end of the week — time to kick back with a Kendall-Jackson Vineyards and Winery 2005 Cabernet Franc Vintners Reserve. At $19, it's an awesome example of just how good this varietal can be. To celebrate the end of a really rough week, try the Owen Roe Cabernet Franc Rosa Mystica Block Yakima Valley 2005, described as having "juicy cherry and herb character" and retailing for about $50.

High roller wines. If you're willing to shell out a few more bucks for something truly special, we recommend either a recent vintage from La Jota (the 2001 is listed at about $60) or a 2003 Cabernet Franc from Pride Mountain Vineyards, a blend of 75 percent Cabernet Franc and 25 percent Merlot, for about $65. The Pride Mountain offers "aromas and flavors of boysenberry, red currant, and fresh sage, followed by ripe blueberry, espresso, and deep chocolate." Admit it, you want some, don't you?

NUTHIN' BUT NEBBIOLO

The king grape of the Piedmont region of Italy, Nebbiolo is at the heart of the great Barolo and Barbaresco wines. It's a high-maintenance grape, named after the fog that envelops the vineyards of that region, and it's one you won't find grown much outside Italy.

Barolo wines are big, massive wines that go on and on. They can age for decades, continually improving but not, in the way of most aged wines, getting softer. Instead, Barolo wines tend to become more concentrated with age until, by the time you take your first sip, it seems as if you are drinking the essence of the grape itself.

That's why you shouldn't drink the Barolo as soon as it's poured. This is a wine that has to relax. Take a couple of sips and put it aside for an hour. Then try it again. You'll find an entirely different taste sensation from that first sip. Continue this process throughout the evening to uncover the layers of fruit hidden within the wine.

These wines, as you might expect, aren't cheap (it's hard to find many under $50), but they're worth the money. Reliable producers include Parusso, Marcarini, Prunotto, and Pira.

Barbaresco wines are just as incredible and elegant as Barolos, but a bit less intimidating (and expensive). They're also somewhat lighter, so they're ready to drink sooner. Producers to look for: Prunotto, Gaja, and Produtorri.

When it comes to these wines, pay special attention to the vintage. If the weather was too hot, too cool, too wet, or too dry, it shows up in the wine. You're pretty safe anywhere from 1996 to 2001; however, the 2002 vintage was a real challenge with heavy rains and violent hailstorms resulting in a total loss for many producers. The 2003 vintage was better than expected and the 2004 is getting rave reviews.

NEBBIOLO: VINICULTURAL VOCABULARY

In good years, wines made with the Nebbiolo grape are densely flavored with thick blackberry and red fruit flavors, such as plum and cherry. You can sometimes catch a whiff of violets on the softer side, while the strength of the wine is described in terms such as black pepper, leather, chocolate, or truffles.

These wines often have a slightly sweet taste; they are so dense with fruit that you might feel like you're licking a spoon of jam. They also have a strong vanilla flavor thanks to their long contact with new oak barrels.

NEBBIOLO: BEST WITH . . .

This strongly flavored wine pairs well with the classical foods of the Italian Piedmont region such as roasted meats, grilled and roasted vegetables, risotto, hearty breads dipped in rich olive oil, and strong cheeses. Our favorite pairing is with roasted venison or leg of lamb studded with garlic and rosemary.

NEBBIOLO: WINES THAT JUST CAN'T MISS

As with all the wines we recommend, you may or may not be able to find these specific ones in your neighborhood wine store. Don't stick to just our recommendations; pick up whatever you find and try them out. Just pay attention to the vintage year.

Everyday wines. Whether it's Tuesday or Sunday, the Nebbiolo Dessilani Colline Novaresi offers a good value and good drinking wine for under $20.

Friday night wines. To end the week on a high note, open a Damilano Barolo 2001, about $60. With its intense aromas of plum, vanilla, licorice, mushroom, and cedar, it garnered a 92-point score from *Wine Spectator*. A couple of other good options include the Barbaresco Santo Stefano 2004 from Castello Di Neive (about $45), and a Barbaresco 2001 from Produttori del Barbarasco (about $45). You should also consider Orlando Abrigo's Barbaresco Vigna Montersino 2001 for about $30 and the Pio Cesare 2003 Barolo for $45 to $60.

High roller wines. High rollers can turn to a top-rated Barolo such as the Conterno-Fantino Barolo Sori Ginestra 2003 Conterno (about $65) or Marchesi di Grésy's Barbaresco Gaiun Martinenga 2001 (about $70). If you want to shoot for the top, try the Bruno Giacosa Barolo Riserva La Roche del Falletto, which will set you back around $300, or the 2000 Domenico Clerico Barolo Percristina, which rated a perfect 100 from *Wine Spectator*.

BOUNTIFUL BARBERA

Given the attention paid to Piedmont's Nebbiolo wines, you'd think it was the only grape grown there. Not quite. We can't forget Barbera d'Alba or Barbera d'Asti. They're both made with the same grape varietal; the different names refer to the town in which the wine is produced. We just call it Barbera.

Barberas are much more affordable than Barolos or Barbarescos, with a wide range of quality wines available between $20 and $30.

Unlike Nebbiolo, you *can* find Barbera grapes grown in California. They are part of that state's new-found love of all things Italian, with wines made from Italian grapes such as Barbera and Sangiovese dubbed "Cal-Ital." This movement actually represents a return to California's winemaking roots, which began with immigrant Italian winemakers.

BARBERA: VINICULTURAL VOCABULARY

Young Barberas tend to be dominated by a taste of cherries, while older ones sometimes have a plumy, lightly spiced persona. This is a red wine to drink relatively young, with most reaching maturity within five years.

BARBERA: BEST WITH . . .

Any kind of hearty, unpretentious food, from hamburgers to chili to classic spaghetti and meatballs. But do drink it with food; we find many Italian wines simply sit there in our mouths and do nothing when drunk on their own.

BARBERA: WINES THAT JUST CAN'T MISS

Everyday wines. To begin your excursion through Barbera, start with the low-cost yet great-tasting Renwood Winery Barbera Sierra Series 2003, about $10. The grapes are fermented in steel then aged ten months in a mixture of new and old American and French oak barrels. The result? Strong, fresh berry aromas with a creamy feel and a slightly spicy finish with hints of vanilla. What a bargain! Other good choices include

Prunotto's Barbera d'Asti Fiulot 2005 (about $15) and Cascina Castlèt's Barbera d'Asti 2005, about $17 and very available.

Friday night wines. Give the Pio Cesare Winery 2004 Barbera d'Alba a try. At $21, it's a bargain. Or pick a California Barbera from Seghesio Winery in California's Sonoma valley. Its 2004 is rich with black-berries and hints of raisin, rum, smoke, dust (yes, dust!), and roasted tomato and retails for about $24.

High roller wines. For that special occasion, the opaque, purple 1998 Braida Barbera d'Asti Bricco dell'Uccellone offers a seductive nose of espresso, roasted meats, black cherries, and raspberries with an underlying spiciness. Dense and full-bodied with a luxurious texture, it retails for about $65. For a more recent vintage, try the 2005 Barbera d'Alba Scarrone Vigna Vecchio, retailing for about $80.

SANGIOVESE: THE GRAPE OF CHIANTI

For many of us, Chianti evokes images of an Italian restaurant with red-checked tablecloths sporting straw-covered wine bottles with candles stuck in the neck. The Chianti poured in these neighborhood eateries was red and rough. If that describes your impression of Chianti, we urge you to try this wonderful wine again.

Sangiovese, the main grape in Chianti, finds its home in the craggy hillsides of one of Italy's most famous winemaking regions: Tuscany. Chianti is actually a wine-growing region within Tuscany, and Chianti Classico, from which most of the Chianti in the United States comes, is a zone within the region. You'll know the wine is a Chianti Classico if you see a black rooster on the neck of the bottle.

Take all that Tuscany evokes—Mediterranean climate, beautiful villas, picturesque villages, acres of vineyards, hot sunshine—and bottle it and you have the best Chianti, known as *riserva*. To be called "riserva," the wine must be aged at least three years before release, usually in French oak.

Although the Chiantis of our youth were often acidic, thin, and generally uninspiring, today's Chianti, like many wines around the world, has undergone a renaissance.

WINES TO BUY

If you're lucky enough to find Italian wines called Brunello di Montalcino or Vino Nobile di Montepulciano, snatch them up. These Tuscan wines, which feature Sangiovese as their prime grape, are some of the best in the world. They'll cost you a bit—upward of $50 bottle—but they're worth it. Buy all you can afford and put them away to age and soften (fifteen to twenty years is often recommended). Then decant before pouring and enjoy.

CHIANTI: VINICULTURE VOCABULARY

Wines made with sangiovese grapes are described as everything from light to full-bodied. Part of the reason for the variety is that the grape itself has mutated several times, so various types of sangiovese grapes are planted throughout the region. Another is, of course, the talent of the winemaker.

Generally, however, Chianti is a very dry red wine that, like most Italian wine, is meant to be drunk with food to reap its full benefits. Terms commonly seen in tasting notes include mixed berry jam, black cherries, and chocolate. The wines are typically deep garnet red with aromas of violets.

CHIANTI: BEST WITH . . .

Anything Italian, particularly anything with a red sauce. Try a Chianti with anchovy pizza one night (the wine is strong enough to cut through the saltiness of the fish and pizza) and veal scaloppini the next. A Bolognese sauce, a lasagna, and even fried calamari with a red dipping sauce works well with this medium-bodied, finely structured wine.

CHIANTI: WINES THAT JUST CAN'T MISS

Everyday wines. Honestly, we don't recommend much low-end Chianti. You're better off spending just a few dollars more for a much better wine. One you might want to try, however, is the Castello di Vicchiomaggio Chianti Classico La Lellera 2003, about $15. Tasting notes mention lots of "spicy blackberry and mineral character," and it's ready to drink. Another with a decent rating is Fattoria Uccelliera di Poggianti's Chianti 2003, about $14.

Friday night wines. You have numerous choices for Chianti in the $16 to $40 range. One of the most highly rated of recent releases is the Viticcio Chianti Classico Riserva 2001, a bargain at $22. Another good value: Castello Della Paneretta Chianti Classico Torre a Destra Riserva 2001, about $30 and ready to drink right now. Described in tasting notes as "rich and ripe, with almost syrupy red and black fruit aromas and flavors," this is a wine that tastes much more expensive than it is.

High roller wines. For just a few dollars more, you get a Chianti that is so much more. One reviewer for *Wine Spectator* described the San Fabiano Calcinaia Chianti Classico Cellole Riserva 2001 as one of the best Classico Chiantis he's ever tasted. And it's only $45! If you really want to splurge, go for the Castello di Ama Chianti Classico Bellavista 2001 ($150), a powerful wine with fabulous beauty and finesse. This wine should just be coming into its prime and is ready to drink now.

MARVELOUS MALBEC

If you've drunk any wine from Chile or Argentina, you've likely stumbled across Malbec and wondered what the heck it is. It used to be grown solely as a blending grape for Bordeaux, but today it's taking center stage in New World wines, creating robust, earthy vino that sells for ridiculously cheap prices.

Argentina leads the New World pack in production of this wine (sometimes called "Malbeck" on the label) and if you come across any, we urge you to snatch it up. You're more likely to find Chilean Malbec, however, simply because that country exports more wine to the United States.

MALBEC: VINICULTURE VOCABULARY

Wines made with the malbec grape are heavy on the fruit flavor, but often have an earthiness about them that leads to descriptions such as "meaty" and "clay flavors." We even occasionally find a bit of effervescence in some Malbec wines. Deb's favorite word for this distinctive taste and aroma is "funky."

MALBEC: BEST WITH . . . .

Pizza turns up again and again in tasting notes on this varietal, specifically, sausage pizza (don't ask us why). It's probably because the smooth, fruity wine is so food friendly. But we also recommend it with anything that goes well with Merlot, including hamburgers, spaghetti, any red sauce dishes, and, of course, since it's *the* wine of Argentina, red meat.

MALBEC: WINES THAT JUST CAN'T MISS

Everyday wines. The amount of excellent Malbec available for under $15 is simply stunning. There are so many that giving you just a couple of recommendations seems sinful. But that's what they pay us the big bucks for. So here are two we've tried and would drink over and over again—if there weren't so much other good stuff out there! Try the Pascual Toso Malbec Mendoza, which retails for about $10, and the Altos las Hormigas Malbec Mendoza, also about $10, described in tasting notes as a "textbook intro to Argentinean Malbec."

Friday night wines. Start with a 2003 Joffre Mendoza Malbec, described as slightly sweet, with strong blackberry, herb, and pepper notes (about $30). Other options include the 2003 Bodegas y Vinedos Santiago Graffigna Malbec Pedernal Valley G (about $17), with "ripe and concentrated black cherry and plum, spicy dark chocolate, and fresh herbal notes," or the 2003 Malbec La Consulta Felipe Rutini ($20)—"plush blackberry and cherry fruit."

High roller wines. With so much excellent Malbec for such affordable prices, you might ask why you should bother spending a lot for a bottle. Actually we haven't, but the wine critics who have say it's worth it. The *San Francisco Chronicle*, for instance, raves about the wines from Vina Cobos in the Mendoza region of Argentina, calling its $150 Cobos Marchiori Vineyard Mendoza Malbec 2003 "an amazingly deep and powerful mouthful of exotic blackberry, blueberry and plum fruit, with spice and toast notes, a meaty texture and velvety tannins." Another wine from the same winery is the 2003 Vina Cobos Bramare, more affordable at $85.

BEAUJOLAIS: NOUVEAU AND BEYOND

While most Americans think of Beaujolais as the soft, fruity wine drunk around the end of November (often during Thanksgiving dinner), usually within days of bottling, there's much more to this light red wine. In fact, we think it's an ideal summer red wine when served slightly chilled. It's also a great transitional wine for people just making the change from white to red wine.

Made with the gamay grape, Beaujolais is a true French wine. The grape is grown in the Beaujolais region of the country (duh!), but the best wines are grown within ten distinct villages, or *crus*. That's why you typically see only the name of the producer and village on these bottles.

The region, or appellation, also provides a clue to the wine itself. Some are lighter and fruitier, such as those from Fleurie and Brouilly, while others are spicier and heavier, such as those from Moulin-à-Vent.

The wine itself has three major levels of quality: the Nouveau, or plain Beaujolais (described below), the Beaujolais-Villages (grown in one of those ten villages), and Beaujolais Cru, typically a year or two older than the available Beaujolais-Villages and more complex. The Beaujolais Cru can age about five years, but no longer. These wines are meant to be drunk young.

BEAUJOLAIS: VINICULTURE VOCABULARY
Fruit, fruit, fruit. Raspberries and jam and blackberries and blueberries. As this is a simple wine, you'll see it described as unpretentious, fun, and friendly. That's

JUST WHAT *IS* BEAUJOLAIS NOUVEAU?

A really great marketing gimmick. Seriously, though, it's the first bottling of the gamay grape harvest. It used to be made as a kind of "thank you" for the vineyard and winery workers after the hard work of picking and crushing. But someone got the brilliant idea of making the release of this first wine of the year into a big deal, setting an official release date of the third Thursday in November and preventing importers from selling it before midnight on the previous Wednesday.

Thus, festivals and parties have sprung up around the release of the "nouveau" throughout France, and wine shops here tout their allotments. Personally, we find the Beaujolais Nouveau acidic and weak, and would much rather open a bottle of Pinot Noir or Zinfandel to partner with our Thanksgiving meal (but that is just our personal view).

not to say, however, that it can't have structure and complexity.

BEAUJOLAIS: BEST WITH . . .

Picnic and cookout foods. Remember, this is not a wine to mull over, but to happily drink. Give it a go with hamburgers and hot dogs, cold chicken, and potato salad. It also stands up well to spicy Mexican food.

BEAUJOLAIS: WINES THAT JUST CAN'T MISS

We don't list our typical three categories or even specific recommendations because most Beaujolais can be found for less than $10 and you really can't go wrong with any of it. If you're new to the varietal, start with any Beaujolais-Villages from Georges Duboeuf, very available, consistently good, and extremely affordable.

As we said earlier, most Beaujolais is meant to be drunk soon after release, so look for the most recent vintages.

MIXING IT UP: MERITAGE AND OTHER BLENDS

While most American wines are labeled based on the grape variety, some of our favorite wines don't even list the grape on the label. They're blends, and they can have three, four, even five or more grapes all blended together.

They can go by lots of names—including the all-encompassing "red table wine." If you see the word "meritage," however, know that there's a method behind the winemaker's madness.

The word itself combines the words "merit" and "heritage." It was selected from more than 6,000 entries in an international contest run in the *Los Angeles Times* to solve the problem of what to call an American blended wine if it didn't contain enough of one grape (75 percent Cabernet Sauvignon, for example) to be designated as that grape on the label, and to distinguish these blended wines from the jug wine moniker "red table wine."

Along with the name came the regulations: A red meritage wine must be made from a blend of Cabernet Sauvignon, Cabernet Franc, Merlot, Malbec, and Petit Verdot, St. Macare, Gros Verdot, or Carménère, the classic Bordeaux grape varieties. The proportions may vary, but at least three of the grape varieties must be used. For white meritage, only Sauvignon Blanc, Sauvignon Vert, and Semillon are permitted.

One of our favorite meritage stories came on a trip to Napa, where we stumbled into a small winery in the north end of the valley called Vincent Arroyo. A family-owned, unpretentious winery, its "tasting room" is just a corner of the large warehouse where the wine is made and stored.

It's also where the winery's black Labrador, Sarah, makes her home, jumping up on the wine barrels to catch tennis balls. She's so much a part of the winery she even has a hand in making one of the wines. Each year, the owners create several different blends from which to choose their meritage bottling. The wine that most appeals to Sarah is the one chosen and dubbed, appropriately enough, "Sarah's Blend." Having drunk several bottles of this delicious wine, all we can say is that Sarah has quite the palate!

MERITAGE: VINICULTURE VOCABULARY

Meritage wines are about blending the best qualities of the included grape varieties to produce the desired final result. Descriptions invoke the names of various black fruits, including blackberry, plums, and cherries. Also look for hints of black licorice, and varying amounts of violets, sage, rosemary, mocha, toffee, and soft oak.

MERITAGE: BEST WITH . . .

We're beginning to sound a little like a broken record, but the meritage wines really pair best with a nice grilled steak or a simple stew.

MERITAGE: WINES THAT JUST CAN'T MISS

Everyday wines. The Kendall Jackson Meritage, about $12, is the clear winner for this style of wine. It provides a good example of what can be achieved by blending.

Friday night wines. A nice easy drinking example is the Estancia Meritage Red Alexander Valley, which you should be able to find for about $20. Go one notch up the scale and you'll find a pair of winners with the 2001 Franciscan Meritage Red Magnificat Napa Valley ($40) and the 2005 Twenty Rows Grappler Napa Red Meritage ($45). Purists might argue that the Twenty Rows isn't a "true" meritage because it includes Zinfandel, but we aren't that picky.

High roller wines. The ultimate high roller meritages are the real things from Bordeaux (more on Bordeaux in Chapter 8). However, in the United States the 2003 Flora Springs Wine Co. Trilogy Meritage Red Napa Valley ($58) and the Conn Valley Eloge Red 2004 Napa Red Meritage ($58) are certainly great choices.

OTHER REDS TO KEEP IN MIND

Don't pass up these other tempting red wines:

Tempranillo. This is the primary grape of Rioja, Spain, and the main grape in the country's famous Rioja wines. It makes dark, fruity wines that can take on great complexity. More on Spain in Chapter 8.

Pinotage. If you're drinking South African wines, you'll come across this grape. It's a mix between pinot noir and another grape called cinsault, resulting in strong, fruity wines with good flavor and a funkiness that we love.

Petite Sirah. Don't let the name fool you. Petite Sirah is not a small wine, nor is it related in any way to Syrah. It's a spicy, well-balanced wine finding much appreciation by California winemakers. Pair it with gamey meats, rich stews, and strong cheeses.

Mourvèdre: This is another blending grape, originally from the Rhone and Provence regions of France, that is starting to shine on its own in wines from California, Spain, and Australia. This is one of the trio of grapes that make up some of Keith's favorite wines. A special something happens when mourvèdre is combined with syrah and grenache grapes to make the wine typically labeled as GSM.

Grenache. This grape is often used to make luscious, perfect-for-summer rosé wines, as well as some excellent Spanish wines.

CHAPTER 6

CHAMPAGNE AND OTHER SPARKLING WINES

$\mathcal{T}$he wine was garnet red, with tiny bubbles streaming through the liquid to escape at the top. Our guests looked at it, uncertain. It was being served in a champagne flute, it had bubbles, but that color . . . certainly this wasn't Champagne?

No, of course not. Champagne comes from grapes grown in the Champagne region of France, where they would have been transformed from their humble beginnings into one of the most storied liquids in the world. And the wine would have been golden or, at the most, a pale pink. Certainly not red!

But this wine, handed out to our guests at the start of an evening to taste wines from the Southern Hemisphere, *was* a sparkling wine. An Australian wine made from shiraz grapes, it delivered the berry flavor of its origin with the bone dryness and nose-tickling characteristics of the finest Champagne. Much to their surprise, everyone loved it.

And therein lies the story. For years, even as we developed our passion and love for all things wine, we stayed away from sparkling wines. A Champagne-soaked evening long ago that resulted in clothes strewn over the living room and a hangover we'd prefer never to repeat convinced us we simply couldn't handle the bubbles. But the more we learned about wine, the more we realized we couldn't continue to slight this noble drink.

So we started experimenting. The key, we soon realized, was stopping at one—okay, maybe two— glasses. Then we could get the joy of the bubbles without the headache.

We'll bet that, like us, you've also stayed away from champagne. Maybe not because of hangover fears, but because you mistakenly think it's only for special occasions and holidays. Or because you think it's too expensive. Or because you think you don't deserve it. Or because you simply don't know how to choose a good sparkling wine.

We have a message for you: Champagne and other sparkling wines are also ideal for Tuesday night.

Don't believe us? Try this. Instead of your normal end-of-the-day drink, pour a flute of sparkling wine. Sip it slowly, letting the bubbles bring effervescence to your day, your evening, your week. We're sure that, like us, you will find that sparkling wine used as an aperitif stimulates your appetite and provides a mini-celebration of the meal to come.

If you take nothing else away from this chapter, take this: Champagne (and its sparkling wine cousins) works just as well with a hamburger as with oysters and foie gras. You just have to get over any preconceived notions of its "specialness." Heck, it's just wine with bubbles, right?

Which brings us to those ubiquitous bubbles. Bet you didn't know that the quality of sparkling wine and

PROPER OPENING TECHNIQUE

Despite what you see in the movies and on television, allowing the cork from a bottle of sparkling wine to pop out, spraying the wine all over, is not the proper way to open the bottle. The popping releases a large amount of carbon dioxide all at once, leaving fewer of those lovely bubbles.

Instead, take a cloth and hold it over the cork as you slowly twist the bottle (not the cork) clockwise, releasing as little gas as possible and, by the way, avoiding nailing an innocent bystander with a flying cork.

champagne can be judged, in part, by the size of the bubbles (aka "beads," as they're called in the business). Basically, the smaller the bubbles, the better the wine. More bubbles mean more flavor and aroma. Think of it as one of the few situations where smaller is better.

Another bubble fact: There are an estimated 49 million bubbles per bottle. Don't believe us? Start counting.

SPARKLING WINES: REGULAR WINES WITH OOMPH

All sparkling wines start out as nonsparkling, or still, wines. They're usually made from a blend of Chardonnay (30 to 40 percent), Pinot Noir (25 to 35 percent), and Pinot Meunier (25 to 35 percent) grapes. Yup, even the palest gold sparkling wine has some red grapes in it. The winemaker just doesn't let the juice touch any of the red grape skins for long during the pressing and resting period. In fact, in France's Champagne region, the grapes are usually pressed in the field in portable presses as soon as they're picked so the juice doesn't sit near the skins for a moment longer than necessary!

That's why the same areas that produce the best Chardonnays and Pinot Noirs also produce the best sparkling wines. In the United States, of course, that would be the Carneros region of Napa Valley and the Willamette Valley region of Oregon.

The formula for making bubbly is actually much simpler than you might think. It's really just the basic fermentation taken one step further.

Recall that fermentation is the combination of sugar and yeast, which yields alcohol and carbon dioxide. The carbon dioxide (the same stuff that makes soda fizzy) is a gas, which dissipates into the air. And that's where typical wine fermentation ends.

But if you're making a sparkling wine, you initiate a *second* fermentation by bottling the wine along with a little additional sugar and yeast. As the second fermentation commences, the carbon dioxide that's created has no place to go. So it remains in the wine.

As you open the bottle of sparkling wine (slowly, we hope), the gas escapes as bubbles. Voila! The "sparkle" in sparkling wine.

Now, what's the difference between sparkling wine and Champagne? Location, location, location.

Champagne is a sparkling wine made in the Champagne region of France (northeast of Paris) with grapes grown there using a centuries-old winemaking process called the *Méthode Traditionelle*. No other bubbly should be referred to as Champagne, even though many are. Technically, based on French labeling laws, just one in twelve bottles of sparkling wine produced worldwide is true Champagne.

Of course, Champagne isn't the only sparkling wine made in France. In the Alsace region in northern France it's called Crémont. Other countries have their own names for sparkling wine, as you'll find in Chapter 8. The Spanish make a sparkling wine called *cava*, while the Italian sparkling wine is called *spumante*.

A BUBBLY BAR

Looking for the ultimate place to celebrate a big promotion or anniversary? Consider a champagne bar. The Bubble Lounge, at 228 West Broadway in New York City's Tribeca neighborhood, or 914 Montgomery St., in San Francisco, serves up more than 300 vintage and nonvintage champagnes by the glass, bottle, and in tasting flights (typically three wines served side-by-side, usually in two- to three-ounce servings). For more information, go to www.bubblelounge.com.

THE PROPER VESSEL

Although we're going to discuss wine glasses in more detail in Chapter 12, champagne glasses deserve their own special explanation. One of the many pleasures of drinking sparkling wines is watching the aforementioned bubbles. Thus, the glass.

Greek mythology holds that the first champagne glass was molded from the breast of Helen of Troy, the most beautiful woman in the world, because drinking wine was a sensual experience and a "fitting" glass was needed. Later, Marie Antoinette reportedly decided to use her own rather more "endowed" breasts as a mold for another glass, the bowl-shaped one often used in wedding toasts (oh, if the bride and groom only knew!).

However, we don't recommend these shallow glasses. Instead, choose a modern sparkling wine glass, which is tulip or flute-shaped. The long, thin shape not only allows a great view of the bubbles, but limits both the amount of wine that comes in contact with the air, as well as the size of the bottom area upon which the bubbles can form. The result: longer-lasting bubbles.

And while we're on the topic of serving bubbly, a word about temperature. *Please* don't serve sparkling wine too warm. It should be served at about 40 degrees—slightly cooler than most white wines. This keeps the effervescence at the perfect level.

Here's a little trick to insure the perfect temperature: Fill one part of your sink with a mixture of ice and water and lay the bottle in it for about twenty minutes. If you have more time, lay the bottle down in the refrigerator for three to four hours.

CHOOSING A SPARKLING WINE

As with any wine, sparkling wines can fall anywhere on the taste continuum from bone dry to sweet. Unlike other wines, however, it's easy to tell what you're getting. Just look for the following:

Brut: dry with a very low sugar content. Flavors of fruits such as melon and pear often predominate.

Extra dry: not as dry as brut.

Sec: semi-sweet.

Demi-sec: sweet. This sparkling wine is typically used as a dessert wine.

Because sparkling wines are more acidic than regular wines, they can have more sweetness and still taste dry. Yeah, we know, it's confusing. But there you have it!

In addition to the code for dryness and sweetness, sparkling wines and Champagne have their own lexicon. But don't worry: Here's all you need to know.

Nonvintage brut. This is a blend of wine made from grapes harvested over two or more years. It offers a more consistent example of the vintner's style and is meant to be drunk within three years of release.

Vintage. This is wine made from grapes from a single year's harvest. Only about three out of every ten years produces a vintage year. Can be aged up to ten years.

Prestige Cuvée. Only made from the cuvée juice (from the first pressing), this is a single year's harvest from the "best" villages and is generally aged longer than other styles. Can be aged about fifteen years.

Blanc de Blanc. This sparkling wine is made exclusively from white (Chardonnay) grapes. These are typically lighter, crisper, more acidic wines that work particularly well as aperitifs or with lighter foods such as raw seafood (think oysters on the half shell).

Blanc de Noir. In contrast to Blanc de Blancs, these wines are produced from dark grapes and are more full bodied.

Rosé. The reddish color in these sparkling wines comes either from additional contact with the skins of

WINE PIONEER: DOM PERIGNON

Who *hasn't* heard of Dom Perignon? Not the drink, but the seventeenth-century monk who created the modern Champagne. Appointed the treasurer and cellar master of the Abbey of Hautvillers, just north of the Champagne region city of Epernay, at age twenty-eight he had two roles: make the wine and make money for the Abbey. It was a tough assignment: Until he took over, the wines of Champagne had a poor reputation as thin red wines with some undesired fizz. Luckily for us, he changed all that.

Among the advances credited to the monk are using grapes from multiple vineyards in the blending process, using English bottles with stronger glass to allow greater pressure in the bottle, the intentional second fermentation, and even the use of cork (from Spain) rather than the chestnut wood surrounded by oiled cloth originally used for closing bottles.

It is said that upon tasting his first glass using the new method he said, "I see stars." We agree.

the dark grapes during pressing or the addition of red wine. These are the most full-bodied sparkling wines and work well with most foods.

SPARKLING WINE: WINES THAT JUST CAN'T MISS

Everyday wines. Try Domaine Ste. Michelle Blanc de Blancs from Oregon's Château Ste. Michelle, around $10. You can also look to Chandon, Mumm, and Domaine Carneros for good values and great bubbles.

Friday night wines. Mumm Cuvée Napa Blanc at $22 or, if you're looking for a true Champagne, try Pommery Blanc de Noirs ($33). Of course, any Champagne from Laurent-Perrier, Charles Heidsiek, Perrier-Jouët (the one with the hand-painted bottle), or Tattinger are also great choices.

High roller wines. Special events deserve only the best Champagne. Go for the big names—Cuvée Dom Perignon from Moet & Chandon at about $100 a bottle, Pol Roger Brut Champagne Cuvée Sir Winston Churchill at around $100 to $200 (depending on the year) or the 1996 Krug Brut Champagne (if you can find any), at about $250 per bottle.

CHAPTER 7

FORTIFIED AND DESSERT WINES

*I*f the phrase "fortified wine" means MD 20-20 and Thunderbird to you, banish those images now. Those are cheap wines with extra alcohol added for the sole purpose of getting drunk fast. They don't even deserve to be within the *shadow* of the category of wines we're going to talk about now.

What we're talking about is more aptly described as the "nectar of the gods."

Fortified wine is wine to which a grape brandy has been added to stop further fermentation, preserve the sweetness and freshness of the grapes, and raise the wine's alcohol content. To add to the wine connection, brandy itself is a liquor (meaning it has a higher alcohol content than wine) distilled from wine.

The first place to start? One of our favorite after-dinner drinks: Port.

PERIPATETIC PORT (OPORTO)

All wine would be Port if it could.
—Old Portuguese proverb

Our wine-drinking buddy Lauriston Hardin (who helped with a couple of chapters in this book) calls Port "one of the greatest contributions made to civil and enlightened society." Why? Pacing. Unlike a bottle of Shiraz that can be emptied in less than half an hour, Port requires that you slow down and appreciate it, making it the ideal wine for the growing "Slow Food" movement.

Port is not a wine that can or should be drunk quickly or even with food. Drink Port fast and you'll find yourself on your knees pretty quick, spending the following day in bed with a killer headache. But sip it slowly, with the reflection and thought it invites, and you're likely to find yourself engaged in the type of deep conversations philosophers often have. Port is a wine that truly infuses the drinker with its essence.

Keith always recalls the Christmas party he and Debra attended years ago during which he and another friend sequestered themselves in an upstairs study, complete with roaring fire and, over the ensuing several hours, proceeded to polish off a bottle of Port, solidifying their friendship for all time in the process.

A BIT OF HISTORY

Port is a wine with an interesting history. It originated in the Douro valley region of northern Portugal, and the name comes from the city of Operto, the second largest city in Portugal, where the Douro River meets the Atlantic Ocean.

In the seventeenth century, England and France were at war and the English were looking for wines to import to replace the French wines (or "claret") they loved. They traveled to Portugal and, finding the wines of the coastal region of weak and poor quality, continued up the Douro where they finally found the strong red wines they craved.

To keep the wines from spoiling during the passage back to England, the sailors added a measure of stabilizing brandy. Then, being English, they named the wines found along the coast not for the villages in which they were created, but for the port city from where they were shipped. Today, Port and the English go together like eggs and ham. You can't blame them; there's nothing more warming during the damp English weather than a good glass of Port.

MAKING PORT

Ports can be made from a blend of up to 80 grape varieties. In fact, most Port growers and vintners don't even know exactly which grape varieties are growing in their vineyards!

After the grapes for Port are picked, they're placed in low stone troughs called *lagares* and crushed (sometimes by foot) for several hours until the skins float to the top of the trough, creating a kind of "cap" over the juice. The wild yeast on the grapes starts the fermentation process immediately.

Over the next few days, the cap of skins is regularly pushed down and brandy added. The brandy keeps the wine from taking on too much color from the skins (and, we admit, gives Port an extra kick).

After a few days in the *lagares*, the wine is placed in wooden casks to age. How long it ages depends on what type of Port is being made (see the following section, "Common Port Styles"). From there, those wines destined to be finer Ports are moved into bottles to allow a much longer and more controlled aging. The rest finish their aging in the wooden casks or even cement tanks.

This is where the difference between "wood" ports and vintage ports comes in. Wood ports should be drunk immediately after bottling as they won't continue to age in the bottle. But vintage ports—bottled only when the wine is truly extraordinary, about once every three years—continue to improve with age and shouldn't be drunk for at least ten to fifteen years. Many can age forty years or more. Vintage ports are the Rolls Royce of Port: rare and meant to be savored.

COMMON PORT STYLES

In addition to wood and vintage ports, other terms are often used to describe Port, including

Ruby. This is the youngest, simplest, and generally least expensive type of Port. Aged two to three years in the barrel, it has a warm, uncomplicated berry flavor.

Tawny. The name comes from the color, which results from aging in wood six years or longer. However, the reality is that many Ports labeled "tawny" really haven't aged any longer than ruby Ports. While it is difficult to tell the difference in the bottle, in the glass a well-aged tawny Port will have a consistent amber-brown hue and a fresh nose. Ideally, tawny Ports should be softer and silkier than ruby Port, thanks to their extended aging.

Late-bottled vintage. These Ports hail from good years that weren't *quite* good enough to be declared vintage. They've usually been bottled four to six years after harvest and are ready to drink upon purchase.

SERVING PORT

Bringing back our good friend Lauriston, we have another Port story to share. On New Year's Eve 1999 he hosted a special dinner to celebrate the new millennium with six couples and their children (we, unfortunately, were in California and, in fact, had not yet met him). His guests, all foodies at heart, planned the menu. But he planned the wines.

When it came time for dessert, he brought out a Dow 1963 Port purchased in the late 1970s by his wife, Frankie, who used to work at a fine wine store in Atlanta.

That Port was a transforming experience for him, his wife, and their guests, he told us. The Port, as he described it, was beauty in a glass. Even though it was more than thirty years old, it still retained a clear, deep amber hue. It smelled like honey on the nose and even just a small taste exploded in the mouth. Suffice it to say that it was like nothing anyone at the table had ever tasted before.

The only sad part of the evening, he relates, was pouring that final drop (and, we think, the fact that we weren't there to share it!).

If you're serving a vintage Port such as Lauriston

did, decant it first to remove the sediment created during the aging process. Otherwise, pouring right from the bottle is fine.

As with any wine, there are glasses specifically designed for Port. They hold about 6.5 ounces of wine and are formed to concentrate the aroma. Recall that Port is to be savored, not gulped!

And you don't have to finish the bottle. The higher alcohol content in Port means it remains drinkable for up to a week after opening. You can store it in the refrigerator, but make sure it returns to room temperature before drinking.

PORT: BEST WITH . . .

Because Ports are usually created from dark grapes, they work well with stronger desserts and cheeses, such as dark chocolate and gorgonzola. But, really, Port itself is dessert in a glass. You don't need anything else with it. Just serve it at room temperature, preferably during a driving rain or snowstorm as you sit by a roaring fire surrounded by good friends.

PORT: WINES THAT JUST CAN'T MISS

If you're looking for a Port, regardless of the type or price range, you can't go wrong with a bottle from Dow, Fonseca, and Taylor Fladgate. More specifically:

Everyday Port. A good, inexpensive tawny Port is Benjamin Australian Tawny Port, less than $10. Very fruity and enjoyable.

Friday night Port. To celebrate the end of the week, pick up a Taylor Fladgate LBV. Some years are better than others, but this is a very reliable Port priced around $20.

High roller Port. Special events such as getting a new job, paying off the mortgage or that last tuition bill, or retiring deserve a vintage Port. The best vintage in almost seventy years was 1994. If you can get your hands on Fonseca or Taylor Fladgate from that year, you'll spend over $300 but you'll be sipping a Port that *Wine Spectator* rated a perfect 100.

SUSSING OUT THE REAL SHERRY

Outside of Spain, Sherry may be the most misunderstood wine in the world. For Americans, our first and possibly only exposure to Sherry is the play *Arsenic and Old Lace*, where the old ladies put arsenic in Sherry because it hid the bitter taste. Not great publicity for this wine!

So get the idea of Sherry and little old ladies out of your mind. In Spain, Sherry is drunk like any other wine. A good Sherry will be bone dry with a nutty tang, not the sweet and sometimes over-alcoholic versions Americans have come to know.

Consequently, Sherry is underappreciated and undersold—and that means you can get some great values.

A BIT OF HISTORY

Just as true Champagne comes from only a small northeast region of France, true Sherry comes from only the sunny southwest Spanish region of Andalusia and its principal cities of Jerez de la Frontera, Puerto de Santa Maria, and Sanlúcar de Barrameda.

It's a region of the world where winemaking dates back to 1110 BC, one that has been pillaged by a variety of invaders through the years, including the Romans, Vandals, Visigoths, Moors, and Christians. Throughout it all, the natives keep right on making fortified wines. Can you blame them?

THE LANGUAGE OF SHERRY

While much of the world thinks of Sherry as a sweet dessert wine, they're only thinking of one type of Sherry: cream. There are several others.

Manzanilla: a dry, light and pale Sherry with subtle notes of saltiness.

Fino: a very dry, pale Sherry. Best drunk within six months of bottling.

Amontillado: a dry-to-medium dry wine. Aged and matured for eight years. Has a lovely amber color.

Oloroso: a full-bodied, dry-to-medium dry wine.

With the exception of cream Sherry, the rest are dry, high in alcohol, and best suited as aperitifs. They also work well with grilled fish and seafood, as the Spanish well know.

The cream Sherry is a wonderful dessert wine that matches well with cookies, pastries, cakes, and even vanilla ice cream.

When tasting Sherry, you're likely to hear descriptors such as "a sweet, smoky element," "salty, tangy ripeness on the nose," or "nutty." The fruit is often described as that of figs and other dried fruits, with vanilla oak often mentioned. That's because of how Sherry is aged—through something called the solera system.

Sherry never comes from a single vintage. Instead, several vintages are stored in rows of barrels and blended on a continuous basis. For instance, Sherry from barrel A is mixed with the wine in barrel B which is, in turn, mixed with the wine in barrel C. Meanwhile, some wine from barrel C might be added back to the wine in barrel A. All in all, it's a very complex and labor intensive process. It also means that every bottle of Sherry holds at least a few molecules of wine from that producer's very first vintage.

Like all wines, Sherry is best consumed within a day or two of opening. However, because of the extra alcohol they contain, most Sherries can last for two to four weeks after opened if kept cool.

SHERRY: WINES THAT JUST CAN'T MISS

As with Port, your best guide for choosing a good Sherry is to look for the producer. Some of the best regularly available in the United States come from Harveys, Sandeman, Savory and James, and Osborne. Others that might be harder to find include Antonio Barbadillo, Gonzelas Byass, Perdo Domecq, and Vinicola Hidalgo.

Everyday Sherry. Cream Jerez Eva NV. Try this cream Sherry with after-dinner ice cream and enjoy what *Wine Spectator* calls its "bittersweet chocolate notes." About $12.

Friday night Sherry. Welcome the weekend with an aperitif of Antonio Barbadillo's Moscatel Jerez Laura NV (about $22) or Vinicola's Hidalgo's Pedro Ximénez Jerez Viejo NV, delicious and fruity at just $18. Another good choice is Barbadillo's Oloroso Jerez Seco Cuco, dry and drinkable at just $30 a bottle.

High roller Sherry. When you're seeking to impress, go for Pedro Domecq's Pedro Ximénez Jerez Venerable, which *Wine Spectator* tasters call "thick and rich" with "complex fig, chocolate and caramel flavors that never gets heavy or cloying." About $80.

MOVING ON TO MADEIRA

Madeira hails from a little island way off the coast of Portugal, and like its Spanish cousin Sherry, also ranges along a continuum from dry to sweet. Sercial is the driest, followed by Verdelho, Golden Boal, and candy-like Malmsey. The relative isolation of the island of Madeira led to the development of this unique wine.

Back in the days before FedEx and UPS, the only way to get goods from country to country was on ships that made long—months-long—journeys. To break up the journey and restock with supplies (including wine), British ships often called at Madeira on their way to and from Africa, South America, or Asia. The sailors quickly learned that in the heat of the tropics the wines rapidly deteriorated. Ever resourceful, they found a workaround: Just add more alcohol (probably from sugar cane). Then they found that these new fortified wines actually tasted better after a few weeks or months at sea. Thus, Madeira was invented.

Pipes (110- to 120-gallon casks) filled with Madeira wines were sent out to mature on a journey before returning on the same ship to be sold. Today the wines, made with the tinta negra mole grape or the more traditional verdelho, bual, sercial, and malvasia grapes, are slow-cooked over three months to provide their unique, nutty tang. This means they can last nearly forever once they're opened.

Maybe that's why the Founding Fathers celebrated the signing of the Declaration of Independence with a glass (or two or three) of Madeira.

MADEIRA: WINES THAT JUST CAN'T MISS

In the United States, unfortunately, we've gotten used to using Madeira primarily as cooking wine. But unless you're making Madeira chicken or veal, we suggest sipping a dry Madeira before dinner or an aged Madeira as an after-dinner treat.

Everyday Madeira. There are a number of inexpensive choices such as Blandy's Sercial Madeira 5-year-old NV (about $20), Cossart Gordon 5-year-old Madeira Buol Medium Rich (about $23), or Leacock's Rainwater Medium Dry Madeira (about $15).

Friday night Madeira. For just a few dollars more, you gain the complexity and maturity that comes with age. Try a Leacock's Bual Madeira 10-Year-Old Medium Rich NV (about $33).

High roller Madeira. Whether you're seeking to impress or just to explore what's possible in the world of wine, go for a vintage Broadbent Bual Madeira or a Barbieto Sercial Madeira. We've seen the 1964 Broadbent on sale for about $130 and the 1978 Barbieto for about $100.

DESSERT WINES

Throughout this chapter, we've been suggesting wines to drink with dessert. So then, what the heck is a dessert wine? In a word, ambrosia. Unlike Port, Sherry, or Madeira, dessert wines are not fortified. In fact, they often have a lower alcohol content than regular wine.

Actually, there is really no clear definition of a dessert wine. The term generally refers to a sweet, full-flavored wine drunk in small amounts at the end of the evening. Because these wines are so sweet, they will "close the palate," providing a sense of completion and, hopefully, contentment to the meal. That's why you taste wines in order from light, acidic wines to heavy, sweet wines throughout a meal, because of their effect on the palate. Acidic wines "open" the palate and sweet wines "close" it.

These wines are typically sold in half bottles because, unlike most wines, you only drink a small amount of dessert wine at a time. Packaging the wine in a smaller bottle means there's less wine to spoil before it's all drunk.

Now, onto the various styles of dessert wines that go beyond the fortified wines we've already discussed.

LATE HARVEST WINES

Late harvest wines are just that. The grapes are left on the vine longer than those picked for regular wines. This enables them to gain significantly higher levels of sugar. More sugar = more alcohol.

Some of the best examples of late harvest wines are the German Auslese (*OWS-lay-zuh*), Beerenauslese (*BAY-ruhn-OWS-lay-zuh*), and Trockenbeerenauslese (*TRAWK-uhn-bay-ruhn-OWS-lay-zuh*) wines. Each is harvested progressively later, thus the Trockenbeerenauslese has much more alcohol (and sugar) than the Auslese. Grape varietals can include riesling, silvaner, and müller-thurgau.

These are not your garden-variety wines. Beerenauslese, for instance, is usually produced just three out of every ten years, the Trockenbeerenauslese even less often. Reasons include weather vagaries that don't allow for late harvesting, and grapes that simply don't reach the quality required.

Producers to look for include Wegeler-Deinhard, Pauly-Bergweiler, Dr. H. Thanish, Selback-Oster, and Schloss Saarstein.

You can also find late harvest wines from other regions, including Washington State, Oregon, and even Virginia. As most come in reasonably priced half bottles, just grab a bottle and try it. In most cases, they match well with fruit tarts or crème brûlée, but we enjoy them on their own.

ICE WINES

Also included in the late harvest mix, or should we say, *very* late harvest mix, are ice wines. Ice wines (a corruption of the German word *Eiswein*) are made from grapes that freeze on the vine and then are picked (usually between 2:00 a.m. and 5:00 a.m.) and crushed. This makes for some very concentrated sugars indeed. In fact, these wines are even sweeter than Beerenauslese and Trockenbeerenauslese. They're also ideal for aging.

The most common grapes used in ice wines are Riesling, Sauvignon Blanc, and Semillon. Look for notes of honey, apricot, butterscotch, and spice, countered by a crisp acidity.

As you might imagine, these wines are not cheap. Expect to pay $50 and up for a half bottle.

THE BEAUTY OF THE ROTTED GRAPE: SAUTERNES

Who would have thought that a fungus that rots grapes also contributes to one of the finest wines in the world? But it does.

Late in the growing season, some semillon or sauvignon blanc grapes left on the vine may develop a fungus called *Botrytis cinerea*, also known as "noble rot." The fungus doesn't actually rot the grape. Instead, it makes clusters of grapes shrivel like raisins, leaving tiny amounts of highly concentrated sweet syrup.

Once harvested, these grapes are turned into some of the most wonderful, prized, and long-lived wines in the world.

Some of the best examples are the Tokaij of Hungary and many of the German Trockenbeerenauslese. However, for our money, the French Sauternes puts them all to shame.

The first "modern" vintage of a sweet sauternes

was the 1847 Châteaux D'Yquem—an 1847 D'Yquem sold at auction in 2004 for over $71,000!—and the French have been dominating ever since. This domination comes in no small part from their dedication to the process. Making a Sauternes is a study in patience: to leave the grapes on the vine until the "noble rot" occurs, to harvest only those grapes that are ready, to press the grapes carefully, and to follow the fermentation process to its natural conclusion without affecting it in any way (such as arresting it by adding sulfur dioxide).

What makes Sauternes different from any other wine is the clean flavor, complexity, and balance. You can easily taste the honey and peaches of the semillon, the apricot of the noble rot, and the acidity of the sauvignon blanc in a complex yet luscious blend. Overall, Sauternes brings a wonderful mix of acidity, alcohol, and sweetness that lingers long after you've swallowed the last drop.

But Sauternes is not just a dessert wine. In his book *Windows on the World Complete Wine Course*, Kevin Zraly relates a story of his visit to a Sauternes château for dinner. With every course (except dessert!) he was served a Sauternes.

Our favorite Sauternes story came during Christmas 2003. As we do every Christmas, we spent it with friends, including Lauriston (whom you met earlier) and his wife Frankie, in Norfolk, Virginia. Keith was hot on the trail of a 2001 Rieussec Sauternes, which he'd seen advertised in a wine store near Norfolk. So on Christmas Eve he and Lauriston took off in search.

Unfortunately, the store they visited had sold out of

the Rieussec (named the top wine that year by *Wine Spectator* magazine), but a sister store forty miles away still had some in stock. Off they went. Upon arrival, they found the store had three half bottles left—at $100 each. Of course, they bought all three. We've opened a bottle every Christmas since. Ah, great wine and great friends. Does it get any better?

DESSERT WINE: WINES THAT JUST CAN'T MISS

If you lust after wonderful dessert wines, be prepared to make a dent in your wallet. However, we think you'll find the tasting pleasure more than worth the financial pain. Some of the Sauternes worth considering are Château D'Yquem (the best and most expensive in the world), Guiraud, Rieussec, D'Arche, and Lamothe. In most cases, excluding D'Yquem, you can expect to spend $50 to $100 per half bottle.

Here are some pocket-friendly alternatives.

Everyday wines. Washington Hills Late Harvest Riesling at $9 for a half bottle. Very enjoyable sweet wine with lots of fruit flavor.

Friday night wines. With quality, prices move up quickly. A great mid-priced Sauternes is the first-growth Château Rieussec 2002 or 2003, about $35 per bottle.

High roller wines. As with champagne, go for the best, Château D'Yquem. You'll spend well over $100 for a half bottle of a recent vintage (the 2005 is upward of $250) but trust us—it's worth it. As the winery's own

Web site notes, "The amazing alchemy brought about by Botrytis cinerea . . . paradoxically transforms decay into gold."

Whenever we eat out, we always skip dessert. "We prefer to drink our calories," we tell the waiters. If you start exploring the wines described in this chapter, we're sure you'll do the same.

CHAPTER 8

OLD WORLD, NEW WORLD

*B*efore there was Australia, the United States, Chile, and Argentina, there was France, Germany, Italy, and Spain: the Old World wine producers. Today, when you hear people refer to "Old World" or "New World" wines, they're talking not only about the country of origin, but about an attitude that goes into the winemaking and marketing.

Although this is a vast oversimplification, Old World wines tend to be more reserved and cautious. They are food-friendly, meaning they don't overwhelm food, and most benefit significantly from aging. New World wines, on the other hand, are big, bold, in-your-face wines meant to be drunk today, although many will improve even more with age.

Old World wines tend to put the emphasis on terroir (remember terroir? If not, check back in Chapter 1), and most are made from the grapes of a single vineyard. New World wines, however, may include grapes from many vineyards—some that are hundreds of miles from the winery itself. They tend to be heavy on oak (some of the cheaper Australian wines are run through oak chips or dust to impart that quintessential vanilla flavor) and often have fun, slightly irreverent labels.

WINE on TUESDAYS

We don't have a favorite style of wine. We like most wines. There are just certain situations and meals that call for an Old World wine, and certain ones that are perfect for New World wines. As you taste more of each, you'll begin to understand the differences and subtle nuances that make each delicious in its own way.

FRANCE IN FIRST

Obviously, when you're talking about wine you start in France. With numerous wine-producing regions, the country still produces more wine than any other in the world (although probably not for much longer). In the next few years, look for Australia and Italy to overtake France in the winemaking department.

While we're going to highlight a few French wine-making regions, this isn't a history or geography lesson. Our goal is that by the time you finish reading about France, you'll be able to walk into a wine store, head to the French section, and know the primary regions and châteaux (aka wine estates or vineyards) from which to choose a decent bottle of wine.

When we first became serious about wine and joined a wine club, we went to several tastings of French wines. We hated them. All of them. We were used to the heavier, fruitier tastes of American and Australian Cabernets, Shiraz, Merlots, and Zinfandels. French wines, however, are usually lighter (less alcohol) with more complexity. They're almost an acquired taste, like caviar.

Other members of the wine club, on hearing that we didn't think we'd ever "get" French wines, told us to wait. "In two years, you'll love them and be buying all you can get your hands on," they said.

They were right. So if you find the subtleness, and sometimes the tannins, of a French wine out of your sphere, don't give up. Like children learning to like their vegetables, sometimes it takes several attempts before you, like us, "get" what all the hoopla is about.

DECIPHERING A FRENCH WINE LABEL

You'll know you're dealing with a French wine if you find the label confusing. (Okay, Germany is probably just as bad, as you'll see in a minute.) In fact, one of the most intimidating things about French wine is the label! Get past that and you're golden.

The first thing to understand is the wine grade. French law is very strict on French wine. The wine must be identified as one of four grades, or quality:

Appellation d'Origine Contrôlée (AOC): the best of the best.

Appellation d'Origine Vin De Qualité Supérieure (AOVDQS): one notch down but still an excellent wine.

Vin de Pays: ordinary drinking wine. Literally translated as "country wine."

Vin de Table: table wine that could be mistaken for vinegar if you're not careful.

Other Frenchisms you should know:

Blanc de Blancs: white wine from white grapes.

Blanc de Noirs: white wine from black (red) grapes.

Cépage: grape variety (Cabernet Sauvignon, Merlot, Pinot Noir, etc.).

Château: the property that made/bottled the wine.

Cru: grown from a specific vineyard.

Cru Bourgeois: classification used for wineries in the Medoc region in Bordeaux (more on Medoc later).

Cru Classé: classed growth, the best wines.

Cuvée: a blend of different varietals.

Domaine: the Burgundian equivalent of the Bordeaux château.

Grand Vin: the château's main wine.

Grand Cru: the highest vineyard classification.

Grand Cru Classé: another indication of very high-quality wine.

Mis en bouteille par: who bottled the wine.

Réserve: a superior wine.

Vendange: vintage. Also called *récolte*.

BREAKING DOWN BORDEAUX

Just as France leads the world in terms of wine quantity and quality, the Bordeaux region leads France when it comes to quality, and some of the finest and most storied wines in the world come out of its rocky soil. These are the wines collectors lust after, the wines that spur bidding wars at auctions, the wines that can break your bank account (and your heart) with a single case. In fact, the entire region is considered the wine capital of the world.

Luckily the wines of Bordeaux, like France itself, are also very democratic. So while you have some magnificent, very expensive wines that take all the limelight, just out of reach of the spotlight are hundreds of fabulous yet affordable wines available to the rest of us.

But with more than 7,000 châteaux producing Bordeaux wines (not of all of them available in the United States, of course), just how *do* you go about choosing? Start with the classification system described on page 125.

THE FAMOUS 1855 CLASSIFICATION

You can't talk about Bordeaux without discussing the 1855 classification of châteaux in the Medoc, Haut-Medoc, and Sauternes regions. Basically, around that time the French emperor Napoleon III asked the top châteaux owners in Bordeaux to rate their wines from best to worst. Since the owners (understandably) bickered endlessly about this, it fell to the Bordeaux Chamber of Commerce to make the final determination.

They grouped the châteaux into five categories, or *crus*, based not on the quality of the wine, but on how much each cost. The system—ranging from first to fifth growths—still persists among Bordeaux wines, giving rise to what wine connoisseurs know as "first growths." A "first growth" is a wine made by one of five wineries in the Bordeaux region of France. These are considered to be some of the best and most expensive wines in the world.

The first-growth châteaux are:

- Château Haut-Brion
- Château Lafite-Rothschild
- Château Latour
- Château Margaux
- Château Mouton-Rothschild

The last on the list, Mouton-Rothschild, was initially ranked as a second growth in 1855. After much skillful campaigning and, we imagine, quite a few bottles of fine wine donated to the "right people," Mouton-Rothschild was elevated to the status of first growth in 1973.

The Bordeaux region makes some white wines, but 84 percent of the wine produced is red.

The reds (called, appropriately enough, Bordeaux), are almost always blends of two or more of the following grapes: cabernet sauvignon, cabernet franc, malbec, merlot, and petit verdot. Until fairly recently, the winemakers of Bordeaux never put the grape varietal on, the label. That's changing, however, as French winemakers find themselves competing with easier-to-understand wine labels from the United States and Australia.

The whites, which can be exceptional, are predominantly made with sauvignon blanc and semillion grapes, sometimes with muscadelle or ugni blanc grapes thrown in for good measure. Most come from one of two regions: Graves and Sauternes (yes, the same Sauternes you learned about in the last chapter).

When it comes to the Bordeaux whites grown in Graves, forget about the growth classification. Instead, look for either upper or lower wines. The lower come from the Graves region and the higher from the Pessac-Léognan region. Within the higher, the best come from one of the top châteaux, including Château Haut-Brion, Château Bouscaut, Château Carbonnières, and Château Olivier.

Sauternes are the great sweet wines of Bordeaux. The flagship wines are produced at Château d'Yquem, the only Grand Premier Cru Sauternes in France. Premier Cru ranks even higher than first growths, wines made by one of the top five wineries. (See "The Famous 1855 Classification," page 125.) Consider it the gold medal in the wine Olympics.

CHOOSING THE RIGHT BORDEAUX WINE

Okay, now you know just enough about Bordeaux to make polite conversation at a cocktail party. Here's what you need to know when it comes to buying the wine: Look for secondary wines from the first- and second-growth châteaux. Same winemaker, same vineyards, but these wines are made with grapes from younger vines or those that simply didn't meet the strict standards for the winery's top blend. That means they cost half as much as the château's prime wine and still taste wonderful. The second wines of the five first growths are

- **Château Lafite-Rothschild:** Carruades de Lafite
- **Château Latour:** Les Forts de Latour
- **Châteaux Margaux:** Pavillon Rouge du Château Margaux
- **Château Haut-Brion:** La Chapelle de La Mission Haut-Brion
- **Château Mouton-Rothschild:** Le Petit Mouton

Buy by vintage. When the Bordeaux region has a good year, all the wines have a good year—regardless of what "growth" they are. So you really can't go wrong choosing a Bordeaux wine from the years 1996, 2000, 2003, and 2005. Stay away from those from 1997, 1999, and 2002, however, unless you're a risk taker.

BURGUNDIAN WINES

If Bordeaux is the home of Merlot and Cabernet Sauvignon, then Burgundy is the home of Pinot Noir. If you ever hear someone say they like Burgundy wines, or describe a wine as having a "Burgundian" flavor, rest assured they're talking Pinot Noir.

The region also boasts some terrific "white Burgundies," or Chardonnay wines, often described as stunningly complex.

This is the area where terroir supposedly has its greatest influence on wine. The region's relatively cool weather, rocky land, and high-maintenance, finicky pinot noir grapes mean Burgundian wines can either be incredible or iffy. One constant challenge is getting enough sun to fully ripen the grapes. Unripe grapes can lead to weakly flavored wines with decidedly vegetal overtones (think cabbage).

TRAVERSING BURGUNDY

Burgundy has five major regions, one of which will be displayed on the bottle:

Chablis. Under French law, Chablis wines are made entirely with chardonnay grapes.

Côte d'Or. The largest region in Burgundy, it is subdivided into Côte de Nuits, which grows only pinot noir grapes, and Côte de Beaune, which grows both pinot noir and chardonnay grapes.

Côte Chalonnaise. This region produces reds from pinot noir grapes and whites from chardonnay grapes.

Mâconnais. This region is best known for its Chardonnays. Not surprising, given that the town of Chardonnay is located here. The best known village and wine from this region is Pouilly-Fuissè, a rich, dry white wine.

Beaujolais. This is the region from which the Beaujolais Nouveau, or the first pressing of the grapes, comes. For more on Beaujolais, check out Chapter 5.

RANKING BURGUNDY'S WINES

Like Bordeaux, Burgundy has its own wine ranking. From top to bottom, here's what to look for:

Grand Cru. The Burgundian equivalent of a first growth. Vineyards in this category include Clos de Vougeot, Musigny, Chambertin, Clos de la Roche, Romanee-Conti, and Montrachet (white). Only thirty-three Grand Cru wines are from Burgundy. They make up just 3 percent of the region's production, but are some of the most expensive and sought-after wines in the world.

Premier Cru. These are high-quality wines, but may be made with grapes from more than one vineyard. There are 562 Premier Cru wines from Burgundy.

Village wines. Less expensive, these wines pool the grapes from a certain village into the wine.

When buying Burgundian wines, look for those from 1999, 2002, 2003, or 2005, and stay away from those from 1998, 2000, 2001, and 2004.

RHÔNES

The Rhône Valley is located in the southeast of France and divided into two parts: northern and southern. Most wines from this region are red, among them the well-known Côte-Rôtie and Hermitage from the north and Châteauneuf-du-Pape from the south.

WINE DRINKERS ASK . . .
WHAT ARE THE RHÔNE RANGERS?

The Rhône Rangers are a group of dedicated California growers who have sought out and cultivated Rhône grape varieties in their state and are now making their own Rhône-style wines. For more about them, go to www.rhonerangers.org.

In the northern region, the grape variety used is exclusively syrah. In the south, the wines are blends, typically dominated by grenache and mouvèdre.

A typical vineyard in the northern Rhône Valley is literally cut into the steep slopes of the valley leading down to the river. The soils are shallow and relatively poor, so the vines have to work hard to produce their fruit. Hence, they don't produce much. But what they do produce tends to be packed with all the fruity, spicy flavors you expect in a big, bold Syrah.

When buying northern Rhône wines, stick to those from 1999, 2003, 2005, or 2006 (although the last two are not ready to drink yet), and avoid those from 2002. Wine from the southern region for the years 2003 to 2006 are all pretty reliable, but again avoid the 2002 (a really bad year!).

GREAT GRAPES (AND WINES) FROM GERMANY

When you think German wine, think white. Wine grapes are grown in thirteen regions in the country, but most are within a few miles of the Rhine River in the southwest corner of the country. The vast majority of grapes are white, with riesling leading the pack. Less common white grapes include müller-thurgau, silvaner, kerner, bacchus, scheurebe, gewürztraminer, grauburgunder or ruländer (pinot gris), and weisser burgunder (pinot blanc).

On the red wine side, spätburgunder and frühburgunder grapes make a Pinot Noir-like wine. Other common grapes going into red wines include portugieser, dornfelder, trollinger, schwarzriesling (pinot meunier), and lemberger.

Like France, Germany also has its classification system. Its great growths are called *Grosses Gewächs*. And if you thought the French system of classifying wine was complex, wait until you see the German system.

Here's your cheat sheet:

Qualitätswein mit Prädikat (QmP). This denotes a quality wine "with distinction." It's the top tier of German wines and is further divided according to the sweetness of the wine into (from driest to nearly pure sugar): kabinett, spätlese, auslese, and beerenauslese.

Qualitätswein bestimmter Anbaugebiete (QbA). This denotes a quality wine from a specific region.

Trockenbeerenauslese and Eiswein (ice wine). You learned about ice wine in Chapter 7. These are definitely worth picking up for some after-dinner sipping.

Deutscher Landwein. Country wine, just one step up from the DTW.

Deutscher Tafelwein (DTW). This is your basic table wine. It's not going to win any awards and can be made with grapes that weren't even grown in Germany!

When buying German, stick with wines from 2001 or younger, with the 2005 vintage being particularly strong. If you look for those imported by Rudi Wiest and Terry Theise, two of the top importers of fine German wines in the United States, you should not go wrong.

INDOMITABLE ITALY

Trying to keep track of Italian wines is like trying to keep track of a bunch of toddlers in a toy store. Simply can't be done.

Just consider the fact that Italy produces more than 1 billion (yes, billion!) gallons of wine a year and you'll understand why.

And don't look for Cabernet Sauvignon, Merlot, and Chardonnay in Italy. Italy's grape varieties are much more diverse. Some estimates put the number of indigenous grape varieties in Italy at between 1,500 and 2,000. After all, the grapevine is native to Italy and is cultivated just about everywhere from the Alps in the north to the tip of Sicily in the south. Also, the history of grape growing in Italy is as old as (if not older than) written history itself, starting with the Etruscans training wild grapes to grow up trees, and continuing with the great Greek and Roman empires tending the vines to ensure a steady supply of their beloved wine.

At the last count Italy had nineteen different wine regions. Those most familiar to Americans are

Piemonte. White varieties from this region include Arneis, Cortese and Moscato. Reds include Barbera, Dolcetto and Nebbiolo.

Emilia-Romagna. White varieties include Albana and Trebbiano. Reds include Lambrusco and Sangiovese.

Toscana. White varieties include Trebbiano and Vernaccia. Reds are primarily made with the sangiovese grape.

Puglia. Whites include Bombino and Trebbiano and reds include Malvasia Nera, Negroamaro, and Primitivo.

Umbria. Look for white varieties including Grechetto and Trebbiano and reds such as Sagrantino and Sangiovese.

When it comes to ranking, Italy is a bit simpler than its European cousins:

Denominazione di Origine Controllata e Guarantita (DOCG). The thirty-two DOCG wines are considered the country's top wines. These include Chianti Classico, Barolo, Brunello di Montalcino, and Barbaresco.

Denominazione di Origine Controllata (DOC). There are 301 DOC-designated wines. The DOC designation specifies not only where the grapes are grown and the types of grapes that can be used in the wine, but even how long the wines must be aged before they can be released. Does this guarantee quality? No, but it goes a long way.

Indicazione Geografica Tipica (IGT). This varietal wine category is similar to the French Vin de Pays (French country wines). There are currently about 120 IGT Italian wines. This really does not guarantee much of anything about the quality.

If you don't see any such designation on the bottle, don't fret. A lot of winemakers couldn't care less about governmental designations; they just want to make good wine.

Other words you might see on Italian wines include

Bianco: white.
Chiaretto: rosé.
Dolce: sweet.
Rosso: red.
Secco: dry.
Spumante: sparkling (the "champagne" of Italy).

STUPENDOUS SPAIN

Spanish winemakers do not make wine—they *elaborar* (elaborate) their wines in wineries called *bodegas*. This tells you a little something about the Spanish attitude to wine and winemaking—they take it very, very seriously.

Although Spain has more land planted with grapes than any other country in the world, because of the relatively low yields of many of its older vineyards, it ranks third in total production behind France and Italy.

Most Spanish winemaking regions are in the northern part of the country. Key regions include

Rioja. Home to one of the most well-known Spanish wines of the same name, Rioja is made from tempranillo grapes and aged in oak barrels for, in some instances, up to ten years.

Ribera del Duero. Winemakers in this region make Bordeaux-style blends, as well as wonderful wines from the tempranillo and grenache grapes.

Penedès. This is where cava, or Spain's version of champagne, is made.

Priorato. This region makes some of the best wines in the world from the grenache grape.

Jerez. This is home to Sherry wines, described in Chapter 7.

Like its European neighbors, Spain also has strict laws regulating the quality of its wine. Its five quality levels (from best to worst) are:

Gran Reserva. This is the best wine, aged in oak for at least two years, plus another three in the bottle, and produced only from the best grapes in the best years.

Reserva. This category indicates a good wine, typically aged for at least three years (one in oak and two in the bottle).

Crianza. A younger wine, this wine is aged at least two years, a minimum of six months in oak.

Vino joven. An even younger wine, this wine *may* be aged just a bit in the barrel, but there's no guarantee.

Vino de mesa. Table wine (stay away!).

Don't be flummoxed by a Spanish wine label. Just use this handy list of common terms:

Blanco: white wine.

Cava: sparkling wines made in the same way as French Champagne.

Clarete: light red wine.

Rosado: rosé.

Tinto: red wine.

HAIL FROM DOWN UNDER: AUSTRALIA

So now we come to the New World. If France is the *grande dame* of wine, then Australia is the college friend who crashes the party and steals her husband. It's from this friendly continent that we have the ubiquitous Yellow Tail wines. There's definitely no challenge to interpreting the wine labels of Aussie wines!

Today, Australia boasts more than 1,900 wineries and is the talisman of the New World philosophy of winemaking—oaky, heavy, and relatively similar.

The vast majority of Australian wines are ready to drink as soon as you get them home and are reasonably priced. They may not impress any wine snobs, but they sure are fun to drink! It's no wonder that they have been steadily gaining in popularity in the United States, with millions of gallons exported every year.

Although the labels might be different, much Australian wine exported to this country comes from one of several large wineries. Pick a wine from one of the following and you can't go wrong: Penfold's, Lindeman, Hardy's, Leewin Estates, Elderton, d'Arenberg, Torbreck, Two-Hands, Wolf Blass, Greg Norman Estates (yes, the golfer), Rosemount Estates, and Wyndam Estates.

And keep in mind that Australia does boast some serious wines that age well and can rightfully take their place in a serious wine collection. The most famous is Penfold's Grange, the "first growth" of Australia. A bottle of the latest vintage can cost upward of $250. In January 2008 we opened a bottle of 1996 Grange to celebrate our seventeenth anniversary. To be honest, we were a little nervous. This type of wine is truly a once-a-decade treat for us. What if it was too soon to drink? What if it didn't taste like a $250 wine? What if it tasted like every other Shiraz from Australia?

We needn't have worried. It was a wonderful, complex, silky smooth wine with abundant dark berry flavors and a finish that lasted for minutes. Seriously, very long, very sublime minutes.

NEW ZEALAND: BEYOND SAUVIGNON BLANC

We've already talked about the amazing Sauvignon Blanc coming out of New Zealand, but don't stop there. Today the country has more than 500 wineries and is expanding from Sauvignon Blanc (which makes up 46 percent of its production) to Chardonnay (22 percent), Pinot Noir (10 percent), and Merlot (7 percent).

But we predict that Pinot Noir will become the dominant red wine for New Zealand in the not-too-distant future. Why? Strong investment and the type of cool climates in which pinot grapes thrive.

Even today there are plenty of New Zealand Pinot Noirs to choose from, particularly from the Craggy Range, Felton Road, and Amisfield wineries.

Regardless of varietal, most New Zealand wines on the market today are meant to be drunk while they are still young and fresh, so grab a bottle of the 2006 or 2007 vintages.

SIPS FROM SOUTH AFRICA

You might not think wine when you think South Africa, but this country has a long history of winemaking, dating back to Dutch colonial times when the colonists vinified wild grapes they found growing around the southern Cape. It wasn't until the demise of apartheid in 1991, however, that South African wines began showing up on U.S. store shelves.

Most South African wines are labeled by grape variety. Wine bearing the name of a particular varietal must contain at least 75 percent of that grape. Most of the classic grape varieties are now grown in South Africa, but its "signature" red varietal is pinotage, briefly discussed in Chapter 5. South Africa is also strong in the white wine department, making some great Chenin Blancs and Sauvignon Blancs.

Reliable whites come from Fairview (Sauvignon Blanc) and Helderberg Winery (Chenin Blanc). Other good values on the red side are Cabernet Sauvignon from Simonsig Wine Estate and the excellent blend called Fusion V from De Toren.

And don't forget one of our favorites: Goats do Roam from Fairview, a spicy blend of several red varietals that's worth drinking every night, particularly at a price under $10.

ARGENTINA: MORE THAN JUST VALUE WINES?

If you need any evidence that Argentina is taking its rightful place among wine-producing countries, look no further than *Wine Enthusiast*. The magazine rated the Pascual Toso 2006 Maipu Vineyards Malbec (Mendoza) the number one wine among its top 100 best buys of 2007. The cost? Just $12.

Like most wine countries, Argentina is split into several wine-producing regions. The major ones are

Mendoza. This is by far the dominant region, accounting for more than 80 percent of Argentina's total wine production. Major varietals include Chardonnay, Cabernet Sauvignon, Merlot, Syrah, and Malbec.

Salta. This region in the far northern part of the country produces some fine Cabernet Sauvignons.

Rio Negro. This region is in the southern part of the country near Patagonia. It is an up-and-coming region for cool climate wines such as Sauvignon Blanc and Pinot Noir. You can also find sparkling wines being made there in collaboration with some of the big French Champagne houses.

San Juan and La Rioja. These two older regions just north of Mendoza produce numerous wines. However, they're mostly for local consumption and are rarely exported.

CHILEAN WINES COME OF AGE

The conquistadores brought wine grapes to Chile in the mid-sixteenth century, but only in the past twenty years has the country focused on wine production — and only in the past ten have we seen any significant amount turning up on our shelves.

Taking a page from the French, in 1994 the Chilean

government defined several appellations, or wine regions. Each is known for the valley in which it resides. The vast majority of Chilean wines we see in the United States come from the Aconcagua, Maipo, and Rapel regions in the northern part of the country. In the south, the focus is on Pinot Noir, Riesling, and other cooler climate wines.

One varietal for which Chile is becoming known—but of which few Americans have heard—is Carménère. Originally grown in the Bordeaux region of France where it is still used as a blending grape, the heat of northern Chile has brought it into its own. Pick up a bottle of Chilean Carménère and you get a glass of deep, smoky, peppery, dark fruit with a long finish and good balance between fruit and tannin that is just perfect for cold winter nights and stews.

Concha y Toro remains one of the most reliable producers and exporters in Chile, producing a range of products from value wines such as the Carménère Rapel Valley Casillero del Diablo 2004 ($9) to the high-end Don Melchar 2002 (about $65). A joint venture between Baroness Philippine de Rothschild of first-growth fame and Concha y Toro created the Viña Almaviva winery. Its 2003 Viña Almaviva Puente Alto ($85) is a winner.

Other highly visible value producers include Casa Lapostolle and Viña Errázuriz.

BRINGING IT HOME: WINE FROM THE UNITED STATES

Of course, we can't talk about New World wines without talking about American wines. The oldest active winery in the United States is thought to be the Brotherhood winery in New York's Hudson Valley, which released its first vintage in 1839.

Today, California is synonymous with the wine industry in the United States, producing about 90 percent of commercial U.S. wines. Although wine is grown throughout the state, perhaps the best-known regions are the Napa and Sonoma valleys northeast of San Francisco—Mecca to wine lovers. Yet believe it or not, they are still rather young when it comes to winemaking regions. In 1960 Napa had just ten wineries; today it boasts more than 250 and fourteen appellations of its own.

But California is far from the only major wine-growing state. Following close behind are Washington, New York, Oregon, Ohio, and Pennsylvania. In fact, every state in the country—including Alaska and Hawaii (pineapple wine, anyone?)—now has at least one commercial winery.

Altogether, the United States boasts 2,400 commercial wineries. So when you travel, we urge you to pick up a couple of bottles of wine from the state you're visiting. You might just be surprised by the quality!

CHAPTER 9

THE MAGICAL PAIRING: WINE AND FOOD

*A*lthough we love sipping our Pinot before and after dinner, the reality is that wine is designed to go with food. That's probably one reason researchers find that wine drinkers tend to be healthier than people who drink other types of alcohol—wine drinkers are more likely to have wine with a meal. So they drink more slowly and usually less than someone working his or her way through a six-pack or a couple of martinis.

We hate to keep bringing up the *Sideways* movie (if you haven't seen it by now, what are you waiting for?), but it simply offers so many classic scenes for the wine lover. Such as when Miles, the protagonist, finally decides to open the rare bottle of Château Cheval Blanc 1961 St.-Emilion Grand Cru (one of the finest wines of the Baby Boomer generation) he's been saving for years.

Does he carefully pour it into fine crystal stemware? Enjoy it with a gourmet meal of veal shanks or braised duck in a setting with fine linen and porcelain plates? Nope. He unceremoniously pours it into a paper cup at his favorite dive and sips it as he munches on a greasy cheeseburger and onion rings.

The message: A great wine is a great wine—

regardless of what it's served with. Our message, however, takes that advice one step further: While a great wine is a great wine regardless of what it's served with, a great meal can make a so-so wine good and a good wine great. Conversely, a great wine can turn even a greasy hamburger into a meal fit for a king.

Here's why.

THE BEAUTY OF WINE AND FOOD

Before we get too far into this chapter, we want to make one thing perfectly clear: There are no hard and fast rules when it comes to wine and food pairing. Oh, sure, we're not going to recommend a heavy red Zinfandel with a delicate sautéed brook trout, but that's because such a pairing would oppose one of our ten guidelines for food/wine pairings (which you'll find on the following pages).

We say "guidelines" rather than rules because that's what they are: parameters to help you make your own decisions about which wine to serve with which foods based on your own personal tastes.

Wine and food are meant to be paired together because each complements the other. The smokiness of a wine may enhance the smokiness of those ribs you just grilled. The acids in a Riesling will counter the creaminess of oysters Rockefeller. Meanwhile, the fruitiness of Chianti enhances the sweetness of a thick spaghetti sauce. It's as if the wine were a condiment, a spice, designed to improve and expose the flavors of the food.

But the pairing works the other way around, too.

The food brings out subtleties in the wine you may never have realized existed. Italian wines are perfect for this. Drunk on their own, many taste too acidic and flat to us. But pair them with a rich pasta dish or a pork roast stuffed with spinach and provolone, and the harshness of the wine smoothes out like a well-ironed tablecloth.

Some winemakers make it easy for you to figure out what goes with what. The River Wild Winery in Arroyo Grande, California, for instance, partnered with Mossy Oak, a hunting gear company, to develop wines just for hunters.

WINE PIONEER: AUGUST ESCOFFIER

A pioneer in the development of fine dining, August Escoffier (1846–1935) was known as the "King of Chefs and the Chef of the Kings." He created such classic foods as Peach Melba and Melba toast, both named after the same famous singer, Nellie Melba.

Escoffier ran the kitchen at London's Savoy and Carlton hotels and in 1898 helped open the famous Ritz Hotel in Paris, with more than 180,000 bottles of cellared wine. It is said that Escoffier first decreed that Burgundy (or red wines) be paired with red meats, and Champagne (later extended to white wines) be paired with fowl and fish.

Today, of course, we know that's not necessarily the case. Just as we feel free to wear white after Labor Day and to mix prints in our wardrobe, we feel free to choose a wine for a meal based on the characteristics of the wine and food—not the color.

Its Wild Game Blends are meant to be paired with wild game, such as waterfowl, wild turkey, and venison, and sport labels with the appropriate animal for pairing. Many other winemakers recommend pairings for their wares on the bottle's labels. And even magazines are jumping into the trend. *Food and Wine* magazine recommends a specific wine for every recipe, and *Better Homes and Gardens* has begun offering wine recommendations for many of its recipes.

But what if there isn't a picture of the food that should be served on the wine's label? How do you learn all this? The same way you learn anything about wine: Experiment!

GORDON GUIDELINES TO PAIRING WINE WITH FOOD

1. Think personality. A heavier wine works best with heavier foods. You wouldn't serve a strong, tannic Cabernet with a delicate vichyssoise. Neither would a delicate Sauvignon Blanc be the ideal choice for a hearty steak. Try to pick a wine that can "take on" the food without over- or under-whelming it.

2. Find complementary characteristics. The wine and food shouldn't be identical. If you're serving duck with a raspberry sauce, a wine with strong overtones of raspberry will get lost. Same for buttery sauces served with buttery Chardonnays. Instead, pair a buttery

sauce with a more acidic wine and that buttery Chard with some spicy crab cakes.
Similarly, sweet dishes make sweet wines
taste bitter (with the notable exception of
dark chocolate and Cabernet Sauvignon or
tawny Port), while salty dishes cry out for the
sweetness of a Mosel Riesling or late harvest
Zinfandel. Don't believe us? Try a piece of
blue cheese with a dessert wine.

3.   Focus on character, not color. Just because
     the food is red doesn't mean the wine has to
     be. For instance, we love a fruity Pinot Noir
     with salmon, particularly if we've basted our
     fish with teriyaki sauce. The berry flavors of
     the Pinot work nicely with the creamy fish,
     all set off by the salty sauce.

4.   Experiment. Just because we said a Pinot
     would go nicely with that salmon doesn't
     mean that's the only thing Keith pulls out of
     the cellar on fish nights. He's just as likely to
     bring up a Riesling, a fruity Grenache, or
     even a Zinfandel. Only if we find that one of
     these wines simply doesn't work with the
     food—and that's all a matter of opinion—do
     we cross it off our list. You should do the
     same. And when you find a great match,
     write it down.

5.   Start light and move to heavy. If you're serv-
     ing several courses with different wines for
     each course, start with lighter wines and
     move toward heavier wines. Consider a
     sparkling wine or even a chilled rosé with

that first course of sautéed shrimp. A Chardonnay might be best with the soup, a Cabernet with the meat, and a Shiraz with the cheese course. This way you don't overwhelm your palate with heavier wines early in the evening.

6. Watch the tannins. A tannic wine (one that makes your mouth pucker slightly) works best with salty, sour, or bitter foods, which soften the tannins and lend a patina of sweetness to the wine.

7. Consider how the food was prepared. Anything grilled or roasted benefits from a stronger, heavier wine, primarily a red. Poached or steamed foods, however, cry out for more delicate whites, rosés, or soft reds.

8. Pay attention to the alcohol content. The higher the alcohol, the bigger the wine. "Bigger" in winespeak means full of fruit and flavor, strong enough to drink on its own, and capable of overwhelming food with its bold aroma and tastes. Wines high in alcohol content need to be paired with dishes that have their own strengths. We're talking hearty meats, red sauces, and thick stews. We are *not* talking veal piccata.

9. Map your wine and food. It makes sense that an Italian Barbaresco would work with spaghetti Bolognese; after all, they hail from the same geographic zone. It's why Gewürztraminers and Rieslings go so well with weiner schnitzel.

10. Relax! If, after the first sip, you realize you made a mistake, open another bottle of wine! This not a life-or-death decision. It's only dinner!

MATCHING WINES TO ETHNIC FOOD

Consider this: The United States has more Chinese restaurants than McDonald's, Wendy's, and Burger King combined, according to the Institute of Food Technologists. And when we head out to eat or order in, our top choice is likely to be Italian (all that pizza), followed by Mexican.

Nowhere does our country's underpinning as a melting pot of cultures become as obvious as when it comes to food. Today, nearly any town large or small sports not only the requisite Chinese, Italian, and Mexican restaurants, but also Thai, Argentinian, Japanese, and Indian cuisines.

And if we're not eating these ethnic delicacies outside our home, we're preparing them ourselves from the plethora of ethnic recipe books jamming bookstore shelves.

So if you thought it was difficult to pick a wine to go with roast chicken, what about pad thai and chimichangas? Read on.

WINE FOR CHINESE FOOD

Certainly you can go with a Chinese wine: plum, lychee, or even honey grape. But we think they're a bit, um, sweet for the sweetness of many Chinese dishes. But we hear the Chinese wine industry is revving up just like every other industry in that powerhouse country. We wouldn't be surprised if in ten years wine stores devote entire sections to Chinese varietals.

Back to the food dilemma, however. Spicy dishes pair well with the acids and spice in Gewürztraminer. For more subtle dishes, such as those in the Cantonese style with brown sauces, balance the saltiness with some sweetness, as in a Riesling or Beaujolais. If you're choosing lots of fried foods, pick a wine with big tannins, such as a Bordeaux or Cabernet Sauvignon, to cut through the greasiness.

WINE DRINKERS ASK . . . WHAT SHOULD I SERVE WITH SALADS?

Pairing wine with salads is tough, especially if you're serving a vinegar-based dressing. The acids in the wine and vinegar compete with one another and both lose. Try using creamy dressings such as blue cheese and ranch with salads and pair with Sauvignon Blanc, Pinot Grigio, or a sparkling wine. Or, conversely, use lemon juice in place of vinegar in an oil-based dressing. In addition to vinegar-based salad dressings, certain other foods just don't seem to pair well with wine. Specifically, we have a hard time with asparagus, artichokes, collard greens, and strong curries.

WINE FOR THAI FOOD

If you're ordering the hottest item on the menu, stick to beer. The spiciness is going to overwhelm any wine you try.

Having said that, if you can bear to order more moderate dishes, wine lovers often recommend Gewürztraminer, whose acidity and sweetness work well with the spicy, salty, earthy flavors of most Thai foods.

Other options include an unoaked Chardonnay or any Sauvignon Blanc, which provide a light foil for the strong flavors of Thai.

WINE FOR JAPANESE FOOD

Japanese food is all over the map. If your pleasure is sushi or sashimi, try a fruity (not too oaky) Chardonnay. The wine is powerful enough to counter the spiciness of the wasabi and saltiness of the soy, but not too overwhelming for the rice and fish. We also think Champagne pairs perfectly.

With tempura, again we'd recommend a wine with some tannins to balance the breading. But if Bordeaux isn't your thing, try a powerful Merlot or red Zinfandel.

And don't be afraid to order a small sampling of the famous Japanese sake, or rice wine. Order it cool, not hot. (Note that sake is meant to be drunk soon after brewing. Unlike grape wines, sake doesn't improve with age.)

WINE FOR MEXICAN FOOD

Mexican food just cries out for beer. But beer makes us bloated. So with this powerfully spiced food, you need an equally powerful wine. Two options immediately come to mind: an intense Zinfandel (any with the Rosenblum label) or a fruity meritage blend. You might also try wines from other countries that mimic Mexican foods, such as Chile and Spain.

Stay away from highly tannic wines, which don't match well with Mexican spiciness.

WINE FOR INDIAN FOOD

The problem with choosing a wine for Indian food is that you have such a mélange of flavors and textures on the plate. But there is a richness to Indian food we think works well with a Pinot Gris or Riesling. And, of course, a Gewürztraminer, which is often considered the only wine for Indian food.

However, we'd never limit ourselves to just one wine with a cuisine, particularly a cuisine as varied as Indian. Try a light Merlot or Beaujolais (even a rosé) with Tandoori-baked dishes and Shiraz/Grenache blends with spicier dishes.

SPARKLING WINES AND FOOD

As you learned in Chapter 6, sparkling wines shouldn't be relegated to special occasions and holidays, but should be a part of normal life for any wine drinker. That means pairing them with food.

In his classic book *Windows on the World Complete Wine Course*, author Kevin Zraly quotes Claude Taittinger's general rule about sparkling wine: "Never with sweets." If you remember just one rule from this book, remember this one.

Instead, pair sparkling wines with seafood or even moderately spicy Asian dishes. Additionally, a more

WHEN IN DOUBT . . .

When you don't know what to choose, go with a sparkling wine, Riesling, or Pinot Noir. All tend to go well with nearly any type of food.

full-bodied Champagne works well with most poultry as well as fried foods, because the acidity in the wine helps counter that greasy feel.

And—one of our favorites—try a good Champagne with strawberries. Decadent and delicious all at once.

BRINGING WINE TO A DINNER PARTY

So you've been invited to dinner at a friend's house. When you ask if you can bring anything, your friend says: "Sure, bring a bottle of wine."

You panic. Your friend collects wine like a pro baseball player collects bats. He has more wine in his cellar than you could hope to drink in ten years. And his last family vacation wasn't at Disney World but in Florence. Florence, *Italy*, that is, where he, his wife, and their five-year-old twins toured Tuscan wineries.

You think about canceling, but your wife has been looking forward to this dinner for days. So you gulp and say fine. Sure, you'll bring the wine.

Just chill. No one expects you to lay out 200 bucks for a cult California Cabernet or even more for a fine

DON'T MAKE THIS MISTAKE

True story: We invited friends to our house for a fancy New Year's Eve dinner. By the end of the meal we'd gone through quite a bit of wine, contributed equally by everyone except one couple. Although they'd brought two bottles, we only drank one.

The next day, the man called and asked us to please return the bottle of $15 wine he'd brought that we hadn't drunk. Needless to say, we've never invited them again and we would no longer call them friends.

Moral of the story: Bringing wine to a friend's house is like bringing a gift; it's incredibly rude to ask for it back.

French wine. Instead, go for the surprise factor. Visit your favorite wine store (more on wine stores and buying wine in Chapter 11), explain the situation to the sales clerk or manager you've befriended, and ask for help picking out a unique wine, one your friend is unlikely to have tasted.

This could be a wine from one of the numerous "smaller" countries exporting wine to the United States, such as Portugal, South Africa, or Chile, or a wine made with a unique grape such as nero davalo (said to be the next "big" thing in red wine), carménère, or chambourcin.

Don't worry about matching the wine to the meal; when you bring wine to a dinner party, the hosts are not expected to serve it. Quite likely, the hosts have already carefully chosen the wines to match the meal. But you can be assured that when they do pull the cork on your wine, they'll think of you.

CHAPTER 10

DINING OUT WITH WINE

$\mathcal{T}$here is perhaps nothing more intimidating about wine than ordering it in a restaurant that sports an actual wine list. Except, perhaps, in a restaurant that also has a sommelier (pronounced *saw-muh-LYAY*). A sommelier, of course, is the person in charge of ordering the wine, developing the wine list, and recommending food/wine pairings. Although they rarely resemble the snooty gentlemen lampooned in cartoons, they can still be quite scary.

Relax. By the time you get through with this chapter, you'll know enough to be able to handle a wine list as smoothly as an NBA player handles a basketball.

THE RESTAURANT WINE LIST: GOOD READING IF YOU HAVE THE TIME

So it's a special occasion—a *really* special occasion— and you've decided to splurge at one of the finest restaurants in the city. You know, the one with the fifty-page wine list that sports more than 500 options. The

DON'T MAKE THIS MISTAKE

Never forget that sommeliers, for all their friendliness, have one primary goal: to make the most money they can on the wines they sell. So don't feel you have to go with a recommendation if it's out of your price range; simply ask for something a little less expensive.

idea of ordering from that list is so terrifying that you decide to skip wine entirely in favor of scotch.

Don't do it. Nothing enhances the taste of food like a matching wine and nothing brings more romance to a special dinner than a good wine. The key is going in prepared with a plan while still giving yourself enough room for a bit of flexibility should something really special appear.

Our first recommendation for traversing that mammoth wine list is to have the restaurant fax or mail you a copy in advance. Ask when you make your reservation; most are happy to do this. Some even post their lists on their Web site. If the list is too mammoth for that, stop in a day or two before your special dinner to peruse it.

This way you can take your time going through the list, looking up wines online and in books, and making your decision ahead of time. You can even just hand the list over to your wine-expert friend, tell her what you think you might be ordering to eat (ask for a copy of the menu when you ask for the wine list), and ask for recommendations. Get several, in case your menu choices change or the wine you want is no longer available.

Now when the waiter asks for your wine order, you can whip out the wine list, point to the exact wine you want, and say the name without stumbling (you've even had time to learn how to pronounce that French name).

ROAD MAP FOR WINE LISTS

Here are our top recommendations for navigating the restaurant wine list:

1. Set a price limit. This is critical, as the markup on most restaurant wine lists is often more than 100 percent. That's why the wine you're buying at the supermarket for $8.99 is $32 at the restaurant. This is a wine you do *not* want to order. Why pay four times the price for a wine you can have anytime? You want to find something you don't normally see in the stores, which is a good possibility because many wineries sell only to restaurants—not retail stores.

2. Decide whether you want red, white, or rosé, sparkling or still. This helps narrow down your choices.

3. Further narrow your choice down to a light wine (a Sauvignon Blanc if you're going with white or Pinot Noir for red) or a heavier wine (a buttery Chardonnay or a tannic Cabernet Sauvignon).

4. Ignore the cheapest wines in each category, which tend to have the highest markups.

5. Identify the wines you've never heard of that meet your first three criteria. After all, what's the point in going through all this effort just to drink a wine you've already tasted?
6. Ask the waiter for a recommendation.
7. Regardless of what the waiter recommends, go with your gut feeling. After all, it's just a bottle of wine! You're not buying a house, for goodness sake!

ORDERING BY THE GLASS

There's nothing wrong with ordering wine by the glass in a restaurant. This is a good option if

- You don't think you can finish an entire bottle at one sitting.
- You and your companion(s) will be selecting dissimilar entrées.
- You want to pair different wines with different courses.
- You want to try different wines with the same course.

A couple of warnings: Too many restaurants keep their red wine-by-the-glass bottles at the bar, where they become too warm, and stick their whites in the beer cooler, where they nearly freeze.

If this is how your restaurant has served red wine in the past (or if you see open bottles standing on the bar), ask the waiter to have the bartender put the red wine in the refrigerator case for fifteen minutes to cool it down and take the white wine *out* of the cooler for fifteen minutes to warm it up.

Also know that some restaurants (albeit not ones that really care about wine) resort to cheap, mass-produced jug wine for their by-the-glass options. After a couple of days behind a smoky, warm bar, it starts to taste like weak cough syrup. If this is the case, you're better off ordering a bottle, even if you don't finish it. Plus, many states have recorking laws that allow diners to take unfinished open bottles home.

And, finally, recognize that the markup on a glass of wine is even higher than on a bottle. One glass could cost you $8 or more; a bottle of the same wine might only be $20—and you'll typically get four or five servings of the restaurant-sized "glass" from that bottle.

We know we've come to a restaurant that values wine if it treats wine-by-the-glass with the same reverence as a full bottle. In these restaurants, the waiter brings the bottle to the table, shows it to you, pours a little in your glass for a taste, waits to get your approval, then pours the wine. This is a restaurant worth returning to (for the wine, at least!).

LOOK FOR A HALF BOTTLE

The perfect solution to the "bottle-is-too-much-but-there-are-no-good-wines-by-the-glass" dilemma is the half bottle, also called a "demi-bottle."

Long a standard in Europe, particularly France, more American producers are bottling their vino in half bottles, and more wine distributors are importing half bottles of European wine.

WINE DRINKERS ASK . . . DO I INCLUDE THE WINE WHEN FIGURING A TIP?

Technically, you don't have to include the cost of the wine when calculating a tip for a meal. If you've been dealing directly with the sommelier, however, it's customary to tip him or her 15 percent of the cost of the wine, depending on the quality of service.

If not, we still recommend you figure the tip on the entire bill—alcohol included. Serving wine properly entails a lot of effort on the part of the waiter, including showing the wine, opening the wine, and keeping the glasses filled throughout the evening.

Luckily, more restaurants are also featuring them on their wine lists. At a recent dinner with Debra's best friend (it was spa weekend for the ladies), the two started their meal with a glass of sparkling Spanish wine. As they'd already had a couple of glasses of red in their hotel room (don't worry, no driving was involved), they opted for a half bottle of an Oregon Pinot Noir to go with their meal. And you know, like the smallest bed in the Goldilocks story, it was *juuuussstt* right.

THE RESTAURANT WINE RITUAL

So you selected the wine, sent the waitress on her way to get it, and are feeling pretty pleased with yourself.

Then the waitress returns and shows you the bottle. *What*, you're thinking, *she doesn't know how to read?*

She does. She's showing you the bottle so you can double-check that the wine you're being served is, indeed, the wine you ordered. This isn't such a problem with a low-end wine for which vintage isn't a big deal (remember vintage? The year the grapes were picked?), but if you've ordered a 2000 Bordeaux (a fabulous year for Bordeaux wines) you sure as heck don't want a 2001 Bordeaux (not such a great year).

So check it carefully.

Once you accept the bottle, the waitress opens the wine and presents you with the cork. No, this is not a souvenir for you to slip into your pocket (although you can, if you want). You need to sniff it. Why? The cork provides a good indication of the quality of the wine. If something's wrong with the wine, you'll know it by sniffing the cork. If it smells like dirty socks (and it's not a French Burgundy, the finest of which often smells like dirty socks), politely tell the waiter you think something's wrong with the wine and you'd like another bottle.

Okay, so the cork smells fruity, not moldy and the wine is the one you ordered. Now the waitress pours about an inch into your glass. You sit, waiting for more. After all, you're thinking, you paid for the darn bottle — you deserve more than an inch of wine!

Chill. You, as the "host" of the party (you ordered the wine, after all) are expected to taste and pass judgment on the wine. Pick up your glass, swirl for a few seconds (recall the tasting instructions in Chapter 2), sniff, and taste. You're looking for any signs that the wine is corked or otherwise spoiled. You also need to

SENDING THE WINE BACK

It's rare, but it does happen. The waiter pours the wine, you take a sip, and you know something's wrong. Typically, the wine is either corked (see page 12 for more on corked wines) or has turned to vinegar in the bottle. In this case, the waiter should bring a replacement bottle at no charge.

Occasionally, you may realize upon taking a sip that the wine you've chosen simply isn't going to work with what you've ordered. In that circumstance (and it should be a rare circumstance), ask the waiter if it's possible to order another bottle instead. Some restaurants won't even charge you for the first bottle, using it at the bar for by-the-glass pours. If this happens to you, make sure you leave a large tip!

make sure this is what you expected and that it will go with your meal.

Once you determine that the wine is okay, simply nod, and then watch as the waitress fills the glasses of the others in your party before finally returning to your glass.

Whew! Now drink.

WINE RESTAURANTS

These days, the wine list at a restaurant is likely to require just as much, if not more, attention than the food. Some restaurants have even turned the wine experience into theater.

Aureole, a Las Vegas restaurant, sports "wine angels"—slender young women dressed in black cat-suits who "fly" on a series of pulleys up the forty-two-foot, glass-enclosed wine tower to fetch the bottle you've ordered. Plus, instead of a ponderous wine list, you're handed a cool mini-computer that allows you to search for a wine by dish (click on your menu selection and a list of recommended wines pops up), country, or varietal.

But a great wine restaurant doesn't need such hype to be outstanding. Things to look for include

- A knowledgeable sommelier, chef, or manager who does the ordering and knows the wines
- Regular multicourse "tasting" menus that pair food and wine
- Quality stemware, such as Riedel or Spiegelau (for more on the importance of wine glasses, see Chapter 12)
- Properly stored wine (temperature-controlled cellars, for instance)
- Trained waitstaff who regularly taste the wines with the restaurant's food so they become knowledgeable about the wine list and confident making recommendations

If you want to know which restaurants are best known for their wine, pick up a copy of the annual restaurant issue from *Wine Spectator*, published in early fall. It lists hundreds of restaurants, divided by state and city, that deserve special attention for their wine lists (and food).

WHEN THE RESTAURANT IS BYOB

One of the nicest things about living in Pennsylvania was the large number of restaurants—both fine dining and family trattorias—that were alcohol free but let you bring your own wine. Few even charged a "corkage" fee, an additional charge tacked onto the bill for "uncorking" and pouring your wine.

If you're lucky enough to have bring-your-own-bottle (BYOB) laws in your state, say a silent prayer of thanks. And then follow these three rules:

- Tip the waiter a little extra for the extra effort to open the bottle for you, bring the glasses, and pour the wine.
- Anticipate the menu and try to bring a wine to match what you might order.
- Consider opening a high-end and/or older wine at home to make sure it's not corked, then bringing the open bottle to the restaurant. After all, this is one wine you can't send back!

THE TASTING MENU

One of the best ways to enjoy wine and food pairings in a restaurant is with a chef's tasting menu. This is when the chef prepares a special, multicourse repast and the sommelier chooses the wines to go along with it. Or, in some situations, it might be the other way around, with the sommelier first choosing the wines and the chef preparing a menu around them.

One of the most memorable of such meals occurred on a visit to Santa Barbara, California. We dined at the Wine Cask restaurant, which, at that time, sported a retail wine store of the same name. It was July 14—Bastille Day—so the chef had prepared a French tasting menu.

The first course still remains in our memory: fois gras with French toast. The buttery, sweet tastes of the French toast along with the creaminess of the goose liver were perfectly set off by a glass of Sauternes. We spent about thirty minutes savoring each bite and sip of that pairing, truly understanding why food and wine were meant to go together.

Our point here (besides making you salivate) is that wine and food belong together and there is no better way to learn this than to partake of a wine dinner. Many restaurants offer them. The dinners are typically reservation only; involve several courses chosen by the chef, each designed to go with a particular wine; and can last for several hours. Sometimes a wine distributor or winemaker attends, providing information about the wines you're drinking and explaining why each particular glass suits the food so well.

We love these dinners. Not only do you get to try wines you've probably never seen or heard of, but you begin to understand how food—and wine—change when paired with one another. For instance, take that Sauternes. While it matched perfectly with the slightly gamy, creamy sweetness of the foie gras French toast, holding just enough acidity to balance the butteriness of the dish, it took on an entirely new facet when we sipped it while nibbling on a piece of salty Roquefort cheese at a wine and cheese pairing. This time, the sweet wine predominated, toning down the salty cheese and providing a taste sensation akin to the sweet/salty mix of kettle corn.

Debra also can't forget a winemaker's dinner she attended one summer where the winemaker served his mead (a wine made from honey) as an after-dinner drink with a dark chocolate dessert. While she generally finds mead too sweet and heavy, the winemaker convinced her to try the two together. What a difference! Unbelievably, the sweetness between the wine and chocolate moderated each other, so that each was *juuuussst* right. Don't ask us how this works. It just does.

We also think wine dinners, while not cheap, offer a great bargain. You often wind up with several courses, from appetizer through dessert, plus three or four glasses of wine, tip included, for less than $100. You are typically seated at a table with people you don't know, so in addition to the fabulous wine and food, you have the opportunity to make new friends over the long meal.

Finding wine dinners is fairly easy. Start by asking at your favorite restaurant. While many advertise, some spread the news by word of mouth, as they can accommodate only twenty or twenty-five people. Also look for ads in local newspapers. And if your favorite restaurant *isn't* hosting wine dinners, suggest they start. You won't be sorry you did!

TRY A WINE BAR

Where can you go to try three different Italian Barolos side by side without investing a C-spot? A wine bar, of course! Wine bars, restaurants, or bars where you can get dozens, even hundreds of wines by the glass, often tasting them side by side, are the hottest thing these days.

They're great for people just learning about wine. Not only can you order excellent wines by the glass, but you can get flights of wine, two- to three-ounce samplings of three to five different wines, usually with a common theme.

Most wine bars also serve food, often tapas, or small, appetizer-sized portions. This is also a treat, as it enables you to taste how the wine changes with different foods. Most cities and towns now sport at least one wine bar; find one to try this weekend!

CHAPTER 11

TIME TO SHOP—FOR WINE

*T*o drink wine, you first have to buy wine. Today, depending on which state you live in, you can buy wine everywhere from your local liquor store and dedicated wine store to the grocery and drugstore down the road.

Even better are new types of wine stores that take the "snob" factor out of purchasing wine. Best Cellars, a chain of wine stores based in New York, is devoted to making "shopping for wine as much fun as drinking it," according to its Web site, and uses the tag line, "Great Wines for Every Day." It offers only quality wines under $15 arranged not by grape or type of wine, but by color and taste, including juicy, smooth, big, and sweet for reds; fizzy, fresh, soft, and luscious for whites.

Another franchise opening shops around the country is Vino 100, which offers 100 wines under $25, rating the wines with its Vino 100 Wine Barometer, from fruity to dry and light to full. Informational labels for each wine tell you not only what they taste like, but what foods they go best with.

Unfortunately, the concept of customer-friendly wine stores still has a ways to go. Too often, you encounter endless shelves of bottles arranged by country or varietal with no sense of what's good, what goes with that rib roast you're having for dinner, or even what's in your price range. When you ask someone for help, you may or may not find someone with the knowledge (and time) to walk you through the various options. Thankfully, you've got us.

WINE, WINE EVERYWHERE

So if wine is sold nearly everywhere (in most states), where's the best place to buy it? That depends on what you're looking for.

If you're in a hurry and just need a bottle for the burgers you're throwing on the grill tonight, then picking up a bottle in the supermarket along with the hamburger buns and extra bottle of relish is fine. Just don't expect to find any good French Burgundies. Your selection is more likely to include lots of easy-to-drink Australians (think Yellow Tail) and California wines (think Gallo and low-end Mondavi), with the occasional Chilean thrown in for good value (think Concha y Toro). You shouldn't spend more than $10, but neither should you expect a life-changing experience when you drink it.

Warehouse clubs are great places to search for that unexpected gem. They sell more fine wines (including top-rated Bordeaux) than just about any other retail outlets in the country. And the warehouse clubs typically only mark up the wine about 14 percent above wholesale. Compare that to the 35 to 40 percent markups in most wine stores. Talk about a bargain!

Some warehouse clubs also stock their own private label wines. We haven't done a full tasting of them yet, but they're certainly worth a try.

Drugstores carry wine in some states; this would be last on our list. Chances are few people are grabbing a bottle of Chardonnay along with the paper towels and aspirin—which means those wines have been sitting there for eons.

Which brings us to retail stores dedicated to wine, or, at least, alcohol.

WHEN IS A LIQUOR STORE NOT A LIQUOR STORE?

When it's a wine store. The reality, though, is that while liquor stores may stock the obligatory red, white, and pink wines, their focus is really on vodka, gin, and scotch. The one exception is states such as Pennsylvania (where we used to live) that regulate all alcohol sales, including wine, and only allow wine to be sold in liquor stores.

In those instances you may find that the state ABC store actually does a fairly good job in the wine department offering, if not the most exciting selection, at least some pretty good pricing. That's because they can buy so *much* wine. Pennsylvania, for instance, is the largest buyer of California wine in the world and the largest purchaser of wine in the United States, buying 6 million cases of wine a year. That lets it buy out most of a vintage at a winery, then offer it to customers for far less than it sells in other retail venues or even in the winery itself.

We used to check out the new offerings every Friday.

The head of the state liquor board would put up specials called Proprietor Specials, at unbelievable prices. Keith would go in, choose a bottle or two of the deals that looked best, then bring them home for Friday night tasting. If they were good, he'd go back on Saturday and buy a case—otherwise, chances were good they wouldn't be around by Tuesday.

Now we live in Virginia. And while we buy a lot of our wine online and direct from the wineries, we occasionally visit a wine store. While we have friends who will drive more than a hundred miles to their favorite wine store and visit wine stores the way other people visit museums, we're not quite that addicted. Still, even Deb will admit she'd rather browse a wine store than a shoe store.

For one, there's the sheer variety. Some wine stores specialize in wines only from a particular geographic area, such as Germany and Alsace. Others sell wines only from a particular state, or from small, boutique wineries. Some are as organized as a scientist's laboratory; others turn every trip into a treasure hunt.

Here's what you *don't* want in your wine store: a hot, dusty environment with a surly clerk behind the counter who rarely ventures out to talk to the customers. Why is temperature important? Because retail wines may sit in a store for weeks, months, even years. If the temperature is too warm, the wine ages too fast. And if it's sitting in the afternoon sun, it may even "cook" and spoil. We'll talk more about wine storage in Chapter 13, but for now, know that the cooler the better.

As for the dust, well, do you think a proprietor that would keep a dusty store would take the necessary care in selecting and storing the wines? Probably not. So why buy your wine there?

In addition to cleanliness and the correct temperature, the ideal wine store should also have the following:

A wine cooler for high-end wines. Again, this gets back to the temperature issue. If your wine store sells really expensive wines, such as a $200 first-growth Bordeaux, you want to make sure it's stored properly, so that when you open it, it still *tastes* like a $200 first-growth Bordeaux. Some wine stores have a walk-in cool room; others store the good stuff in the basement.

Trained staff. Visiting a good wine store should be like visiting an art gallery. The staff there should know enough about the contents to give you a brief overview, tell you exactly where to find that particular bottle of wine, and listen well enough to match your individual taste and price range to the merchandise. If you tell the clerk you're looking for a moderately priced red wine to go with the lamb shanks you're having tonight, she should know exactly what to recommend. Hint: If the clerk says she never drinks red wine, it's time to find another wine store.

Clearly identified merchandise. You don't want to guess the price of a wine or ask every time you find one you'd like to try. Additionally, you don't want to wander aimlessly looking for the Malbec. A quality wine store not only puts price tags on their wines, but has clearly accessible signage directing you to the wines of your choice, usually with ratings and tasting notes.

Case discounts. If you're buying a case of wine (twelve bottles), the store should offer you a 10 to 15 percent discount on the case. It's just good business.

E-mail list. Our favorite wine stores send us weekly e-mails telling us what's on special, what's hot, what's going on. It's a great way to keep us in the loop and alert us to values we might not otherwise have found (and to keep us buying their wine).

Variety. If all you're looking for are low-end, mass-merchandised wines, you might as well pick up your vino in the supermarket. You venture into a wine store for the same reason you buy cheese at a fromagerie: to find the unexpected. So if your wine store seems to stock the same boring producers and labels week after week, it's time to hunt for a new one. Another no-no: wine that seems to linger on the shelves. You want a wine store where the stock turns over so it doesn't get stale or lose its taste appeal.

Special events. Find a wine store that offers tastings, wine lectures, book signings. This is a store whose owner cares about cultivating customers, someone who knows that the better educated you are, the more (and more expensive) wine you'll buy. Plus, in-store wine tastings are a great way to get to know new wines and other wine lovers.

MAKING SENSE OF THE NUMBERS

Walk into a wine store these days and the first thing you're likely to see is a tag on the wine bottle touting a score of 92. Huh? Since when did they start grading wines?

Since Robert Parker, aka "the emperor of wine," came on the scene about twenty-five years ago with his newsletter, the *Wine Advocate*. Until Parker began writing about wine, wine publications and connoisseurs used a star system to rate wines or, at the most, a 20-point scale.

Parker, however, decided that Americans, used to the 100-point scale we grew up with in school, would do better using the same scale to rate Cabernets. Other wine publications such as *Wine Spectator* and *Wine Enthusiast* followed, and today the shelves of wine stores are jammed with little cards that use ratings and tasting notes as marketing tools. Even wine store employees get into the game, providing their own ratings (actually, we'd be more inclined to go with these than the ones from the big magazines).

Here's what you need to know about those scales:

- The 100-point scale starts at 50.
- You will rarely, if ever, see a score less than 80.
- A wine's score often determines its price, so a 100-point wine is going to set you back more than an 85-point wine.
- A wine's score often determines its availability. If you just got your issue of the *Wine Advocate* in the mail and want to order that 100-point California Cabernet, better get on the phone quickly. As soon as the publication hits the streets, those highly rated wines fly out the door.

And the most important thing to know about scores: They're only as good as the paper on which they're written. In other words, the only score that really matters is the one you give the wine. Yet we know people who proudly boast that they never buy a wine rated less than 95. How boring. Don't be like these dullards. The fun of wine is experimentation, and you'll never find that hidden jewel if you never leave the main road.

MAKING SENSE OF WINE SHIPPING LAWS

So you stumbled on an amazing red wine at this little winery in the hills of Oregon and you want to ship back two or three cases to your home in Arkansas. Good luck.

Arkansas, like many states, doesn't allow wineries from outside the state to ship to private individuals inside the state. It's as if Lands' End were allowed to ship its ski jackets and turtlenecks to residents of Maine and Vermont, but not Massachusetts or New Hampshire.

Some states require wineries to have permits to ship into the state; others don't. Some charge taxes, others don't. Most limit the amount of wine you can have shipped from one winery (usually two cases a year), but few really enforce that rule. Your small mom-and-pop winery can't keep track of it all; heck, national wine people often can't keep track of it, either.

Plus, wine shipping laws are in flux, thanks to a 2005 Supreme Court ruling that basically said if a state lets its in-state wineries ship to individuals within the state, it has to let out-of-state wineries ship to individuals within the state. The ruling has set off a plethora of lawsuits and law revisions in states around the country that will probably continue through the end of the decade.

To track the ever-changing world of state alcohol regulations, try the Wine Institute's Web site at www.wineinstitute.org and search for its Direct

Shipping homepage. Another good option is Direct Shipping News and Updates at www.wineinstitute.org. Click on State Shipping Laws for specifics. Knowing state rules is important not just for buying from wineries, but also for buying wine online. And trust us, you *want* to buy wine online!

BUYING WINE ONLINE

Once the Internet grabbed hold in our lives, could online wine buying be far behind? Nope. Today, you have access to the inventories of major wine stores around the country, such as Pop's Wines on Long Island in New York and Sam's Wines and Spirits in Chicago. Every week or so, we get an e-mail from Pop's. They usually start something like this:

GREETINGS!!

On a regular basis we come across new wines, wines of note, wines we think you can't live without!

2004 ROMBAUER VINEYARDS CABERNET SAUVIGNON, NAPA VALLEY, 750ML

They say $30 (New York Times), we say $23+, when bought by the case!!

#2 IN A TASTING OF 25 2004 NAPA VALLEY CABERNETS,

1st place was $40, this was the only other 3 star wine!

*"Nicely textured and well balanced with spicy cranberry
and mint aromas and flavors."*
BEST VALUE, WINES OF THE TIMES,
THE NEW YORK TIMES, ERIC ASIMOV,
JANUARY 23, 2008

$30.99—Good Wine Stores
$27.89—Pop's Single Bottle Price
$24.79—Pop's Mixed Case Price
$278.91—Pop's Case Price

BUY IT!!

How can you resist?

The beauty of online wine buying is that you can search the wine site's database by name, year, even varietal. You can compare prices online and find wines that your local wine store never heard of. The bad news, of course, is that the shipping laws of your individual state may prohibit the shipment of such wines.

One other caveat: Make sure you figure in the cost of shipping and handling for that case of wine. Once you add in these extras, you may find your "bargain' is no longer such a bargain.

A good place to start if you're looking for that one special bottle of wine is www.wine-searcher.com. This site lets you type in a specific wine, even the vintage year, and search databases of dozens of online wine stores to show you where the wine is available and at what price.

Here are some of our favorite online wine stores:

• The Wine Library (www.winelibrary.com)

- Wally's Wine (www.wallywine.com)
- Wine.Com (www.wine.com)
- Pop's Wines and Spirits (www.popswine.com)
- Southern Hemisphere Wine Center (www.southernwines.com)
- Wine Access (www.wineaccess.com)

JOIN THE CLUB–THE WINE CLUB

Looking for the perfect gift for that certain someone-who-has-everything? How about a couple of bottles of Virginia wine delivered to their door several times a year? Or maybe Zinfandels from a tiny vineyard tucked in the corner of Napa Valley that only sells its wine to an exclusive list of people? Perhaps instead of another sweater, kitchen appliance, or perfume you can tuck a flyer for a wine club under the tree.

Wine clubs are a terrific way to learn about and drink wines you won't find in big box stores, supermarkets, or even specialty wine stores. Many wineries, particularly the smaller ones, sell their wines only through the winery or a wine club. After all, if you only make 300 cases (3,600 bottles) of a particular wine, it's not worth the time or money to go through a distributor and send it halfway across the country. So you start a wine club.

Most wine clubs cost nothing to join and provide discounts on every bottle and case of wine you purchase. Typically, you agree to accept shipment of a certain number of bottles every month, quarter, or biannually, depending on the wine club.

Some let you choose the type of wine or the color (white or red); others have a take-it-or-leave-it mentality. Some offer other perks, such as invitations to special barrel tastings or winery events. One winery we visited while in Sonoma, Ledson Winery (www.ledsonwinery.com), owns a boutique hotel on the town's main square. As members of the wine club, we're now entitled to a 10 percent discount on rooms at the hotel, not to mention private tastings in the "club" tasting room, an elegant, wood-lined room with a spectacular view of the vineyards that imparts a far different experience from the overcrowded tasting room on the winery's ground floor.

Some wine clubs are so exclusive it can take years to get on the list. Keith has spent four years on the waiting list of the Sine Qua Non winery, whose wines typically get 98-plus ratings from wine guru Robert Parker. Every six months they send him a postcard saying, in essence, "Ha ha, sucker! You're still not going to get any of our wines!" It's heartbreaking to be around him on those days.

But wine clubs aren't limited to wineries. Many states offer wine clubs to let you sample their wines. Virginia, for instance, has a free wine club (you pay only for the wines and shipping) through its Web site www.vawineclub.com. You can choose one bottle a month for $14.95 or two bottles a month for $24.95. There's even an online form to complete for a gift subscription. You can also find Wine-of-the-Month (or semi-month) clubs, which work just like Book-of-the-Month clubs. We used to belong to Southern Hemisphere Wine Center's club (www.southernwines.com) and enjoyed getting shipments of hard-to-find wines from Chile, Australia, Argentina, South Africa, and New Zealand.

In fact, we find wine clubs so much fun that we tend to join them at nearly every winery we visit. "Man, you people must love parties," the UPS guy mused after lugging a couple of cases onto our porch.

What could we say? For us, visiting a winery is what a visit to a nursery must be like for a gardener on the first warm day in April—intoxicating. The only advice we'd provide about joining wine clubs and purchasing wine at wineries is the same we'd tell you when it comes to drinking the stuff: All things in moderation.

BUYING WINE AT AUCTIONS

Want a fun way to spend a Saturday? Go to a wine auction. Found in most large cities, these are free, open-to-the-public events where you can find unique, high-end wines or simply hard-to-find-yet-still-affordable wines. They often offer tastings of some of the wines that will be auctioned off before or during the event, and, if nothing, else, are great venues for people watching.

We chose Christie's Auction House in New York City for our first auction. Simply by providing our bank account number and first-born child (just kidding about the kid), we procured a paddle and headed not to the seating area where the auction was in full mode, but to the tasting tables, where bottles of forty-year-old first growths were available for pouring.

Our thirst and curiosity quenched, we sat down to watch the action. It was infectious—and quick. With more than two thousand lots to sell (a lot is the unit being auctioned off, anything from a single bottle of wine to several bottles or a case or more) the auctioneers were going through one every twelve to fifteen seconds!

Not all auctions go that quickly, however. Here's what you need to know about wine auctions:

- Get the auction catalog ahead of time and go through it carefully, marking any lots you might want to bid on.
- Set a budget and stick to it! It's easy to get caught up in the excitement.
- Make sure you have enough money in your checking account. Most auctions won't take credit cards.
- Go prepared to learn something new at every auction.
- Try and meet some of your fellow bidders; many are full of information.
- Take advantage of the ancillary events, such as tasting dinners and lunches, which occur in conjunction with the auction. They make the whole experience more of a, well, *experience*.
- Understand that, unlike purchases from a wine merchant, if anything is wrong with the wine, you're out of luck. But auction experts say they do everything in their power short of tasting the wine to insure that doesn't happen. You can do your homework, too, by previewing the wine before the auction or paying attention to the details in the catalog that tell you the condition of the label, bottle, and cork.
- Anticipate hidden costs when purchasing wine at auction. For instance, while you may have won

that case of white Burgundy for $500, by the time the "buyer's premium," the amount the auction house gets, and taxes are tacked on (plus shipping if you don't plan to pick it up yourself), you may find your "bargain" slipping away.

BUYING WINE FUTURES

Why would anyone hand over $300 or more for a case of wine that doesn't even exist yet? Because they're buying wine futures.

The concept is really quite simple: You buy the wine today, when it's still in the barrel, at a lower cost than you'd pay if you waited to buy once it's bottled — if there's any left to buy.

Wine futures are often used to buy fine wines such as high-end Bordeaux from France or to ensure you get a supply of wines produced in small quantity.

Some wine people think of it as an investment — putting a sum of money aside and seeing it "grow" in value as the wine grows in value. But unless you've read a review of the wine in the barrel (called a "barrel tasting") by a reputable wine writer, or tasted the early wine yourself, you're taking a big risk.

Meanwhile, the wine merchant and the winery itself get the free use of your money.

Our advice? Try a high-yield CD instead and when it matures, and the wine you want is also mature, head to the wine store.

CHAPTER 12

CORKSCREW ANYONE? WINE PARAPHERNALIA

*I*f you really get into wine as a hobby, you can spend as much money as you earn. Not just on the wine. Once you land on certain mailing lists (and we're not sure quite how this works, given that our fifteen-year-old son keeps receiving a catalog for rare wines), you'll find your mailbox stuffed with glossy bulletins advertising wine-related paraphernalia ranging from patterned ties to fuzzy socks imprinted with wine bottles.

We've fallen victim to this ourselves. Wine-related items can be spotted throughout our house: prints of wine bottles on our great room walls, two pseudo-aged plaques reading "Bordeaux" and "Burgundy" in our kitchen, and a sign above the doorway reading: "Food is Good. Wine is Better."

One plus is that our friends never have to struggle with buying us gifts. For Keith's birthday, his boss gave him a replica street sign reading "Gordon Grand Cru Boulevard." For Christmas we received a lovely floor mat imprinted with the phrase: "Go Away. Come Back with Wine."

And that's not even counting the drawer full of corkscrews and wine stoppers, and the cabinets filled with wine glasses. Which brings us to the topic of this chapter: wine stuff.

CORKSCREWS

For centuries, there was wine but no corkscrews. After all, who needed corkscrews when all wine came in barrels and no one had yet invented the cork?

But with the advent of glass blowing came the advent of wine bottles. And when you have wine bottles, you need something to keep the wine in and the air out. That's where the cork comes in. First used by the English, who imported the cork from Portugal and Spain (where much of it still originates), corks did their job well, but were darn hard to get out with your teeth.

Enter the corkscrew. No one really knows who invented the first corkscrew, but the first patent on it was issued in 1795 to an Englishman from Middlesex. The earliest corkscrews were made by blacksmiths and gunsmiths. These artisans used a twisted piece of metal used to clean out guns as their model. This twist is still endemic to many corkscrew models today. It's called the "worm," probably because it winds its way into the cork as a worm winds its way through your garden.

CHECK THIS OUT

If you're at all interested in corkscrews, visit the Virtual Corkscrew Museum at www.bullworks.net/virtual.htm. Thirty "rooms" feature hundreds of corkscrews, trivia about corkscrews, information about corkscrew collecting, and even books about corkscrews.

Today, of course, there are numerous varieties of corkscrews, some without any sign of the "worm." Here are a few of the most common:

Waiter's style. This type of corkscrew is most commonly found in restaurants because it slips so easily into a pocket. It's also the one we use most often. Not only is it portable, but includes a small knife to cut the foil around the top of the bottle. To use, unfold the foil cutter and remove the covering over the cork. Then twist the "worm" into the cork until the spiral disappears. Now place the lever on the lip of the bottle and pull out the cork. A bonus: You can use the lever to open other bottle caps should the need for a beer ever hit, and, with practice, you can open a bottle of wine without setting it down on a table.

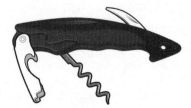

Ah-so style. If you're opening an old bottle of wine with a crumbling cork, or you messed up and the cork is only halfway out, or you simply want to preserve the cork without any holes in it, then use the Ah-so corkscrew. Technically it's called a butler's corkscrew, but legend has it that its more common name came about because when you figure out how it works you go: "Ah, so *that's* how it works." Using it is very simple. You carefully slide the prongs alongside the cork until they are fully in the bottle and the top of the device rests on the cork. Then use a gentle back-and-forth motion as you pull up on the cork.

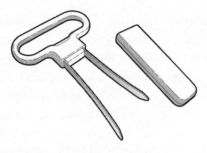

Lever style. Here's where the famous Rabbit screw-pull comes in. The makers of the original Rabbit claim their corkscrew pulls a cork in three seconds flat and can open 20,000 bottles of wine before being put out to pasture. This is the one we pull out when we're opening lots of bottles of wine for a party or wine tasting. There are several copycats on the market, but they all work about the same.

1. Remove the foil wrapping using the foil cutter that comes with every Rabbit.

2. Hold the Rabbit screwpull by its gripping handles with your left hand. With your right hand, raise the corkscrew by bringing the top handle forward and down.
3. Place the gripping handles around the neck of the bottle, squeeze firmly, and center the corkscrew over the bottle.
4. Insert the corkscrew into the cork by bringing the top handle up and back.
5. Pull the cork by bringing the handle forward and down.

Now you have an uncorked bottle of wine.

To release the cork, simply bring the top handle up and back, then grip the cork firmly with gripping handles and bring the handle forward and down.

French plastic pocket style. This is the cheapest corkscrew you can buy—for a reason. It's a pain to use. It's also the one many hotels leave in your room, which is why we always travel with our own waiter's corkscrew. To use this style, wind the worm into the cork until the handle rests on top of the cork, then carefully pull up while holding tightly to the wine bottle. Go slow; you don't want a lap full of wine.

Corky cork extractor. This ingenious system uses a hand pumped vacuum to remove the cork. Simply stick the needle into the center of the cork and start pumping.

WHEN THINGS GO WRONG

So you followed our directions perfectly but the cork still crumbled and bits and pieces wound up in that fine Merlot you were planning to drink with dinner. Or, instead of pulling the cork out, you pushed the cork in. No problem!

Just pick up your handy-dandy cork retriever and start fishing. The wires expand in the bottle and contract when you remove the retriever.

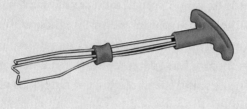

OF GLASSES AND WINE

We've talked a bit about appropriate wine glasses throughout this book. You already know, for instance, about the right glass for sparkling wine (see page 98) and Port (see page 107).

If you listen to the wine snobs, you should have an entire wall of fine crystal—a different glass for every varietal. We say, phooey. In our mind, all you need is a set of decent white, red, and dessert glasses. If you drink a lot of sparkling wine, by all means invest in a set of flutes; otherwise, a white wine glass works just fine.

WINE PIONEER: RIEDEL, INC.

Blame, or thank, crystal stemware manufacturer Riedel, Inc., for the current interest in wine glass shapes. In the 1950s, ninth-generation family member Claus J. Riedel was the first glass manufacturer to change wine glasses from the traditional colored, cut glass to the clear, simple, thin glasses we have today. A few years later, in 1961, Riedel introduced the first collection of wine glasses designed for different grape varietals.

But the crowning glory didn't occur until more than a decade later, in 1973, when Riedel introduced its classic Sommelier series of glasses, still sold today. With seven red wine glasses, ten white wine glasses, three champagne flutes and eight glasses for fortified wines, the line has become the standard by which other wine glass manufacturers measure themselves.

In fact, esteemed wine critic Robert Parker uses Riedel stemware for his tastings. He once called the effect of Riedel glasses on fine wine "profound." He is quoted as saying, "I cannot emphasize enough what a difference they make."

But hey, far be it for Riedel to be snobby. These days, you can pick up a set of their, ahem, lesser glasses in many department stores for under $30.

Personally, we don't like to spend more than $5 or $6 per glass because we have a tendency to break them. We've gone a bit higher, however, since we discovered Schott Zwiesel's Titan Crystal. Considered "break resistant," these glasses are imbued with titanium to enhance their strength. While they look like fine crystal, they're strong as plastic. In four years, we've (well, Deb) has only broken one, when she accidentally smashed it against the refrigerator. Cost varies, but range between $6 and $10 a glass, depending on the type.

In our mind, here are the key attributes of quality wine glasses:

- They should be clear, so you can see the color of the wine.
- They should have a thin rim and a long stem.
- They should be much larger than any glass of wine you'd ever pour so you have enough room to swish the wine around without spilling it all over yourself.

Oh, and one other thing. They should be of the appropriate shape. Because, even though we're not wine snobs by any stretch of the imagination, we do think that shape matters when it comes to wine glasses. Here's why.

First, the glass is the instrument used to convey the wine to your mouth. Just as you wouldn't use a rusty spoon for a delicate vichyssoise, you wouldn't want to use a thick, clumsy glass for a fine wine (or even a $7 bottle of Yellow Tail).

Second, and most important, the glass is vital for the wine. Wine needs oxygen to fully open and unleash its full flavor, which is why red wine glasses have such large bowls.

So here's what to look for when buying wine glasses.

White wine glasses. White wines don't need as much air as red wines to "open up" and the smaller, narrower bowl of the glass reflects that. Meanwhile, the shape of the rim directs the wine toward the front of the mouth, a more sensitive area for sweetness.

Red wine glasses. Unless you're drinking a fine, aged Bordeaux, a classic wine glass like the one shown here works well for most red wines. Note the large bowl, designed to expose the maximum surface of wine to the air, and the tapered rim, designed to direct the wine to the sides and back of the tongue for maximum pleasure.

Bourdeaux glasses. If you're drinking Grand Cru Bordeaux or Burgundies, you deserve the correct glass for the wine. The Bordeaux glass shown, with its longer stem and larger bowl, will serve perfectly.

Dessert wine glasses. Dessert wine glasses are small, designed to concentrate the fruit of the wine without calling attention to the alcohol. The small opening also forces your mouth to pucker up, putting the sweet wine right at the tip of the tongue. Although there are literally hundreds of designs for these glasses, the key is the size. Most hold no more than eight ounces, often less.

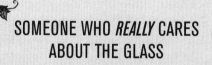

SOMEONE WHO *REALLY* CARES ABOUT THE GLASS

Our cousin Arlene, a retired New York City guidance counselor, admits she's just slightly neurotic when it comes to wine. For one, she only drinks one type of wine–an Oregon Pinot Noir she buys by the case. For another, she only drinks her wine out of a Riedel Burgundy Grand Cru wine glass.

She's so certain that the glass enhances the wine, in fact, that she carries her goblet in a special carrying case to friends' houses, BYOB restaurants, and travel destinations. As she says, "I've come to love the thinness of certain wine glasses, and if I have to drink out of a less expensive, thicker glass, I'd almost rather not drink the wine."

Now *that's* dedication!

FOR THE CHRISTMAS STOCKING

Okay, we've covered the two major purchases (beyond wine) you need to enjoy a glass of the grape. Now onto the fun stuff. The following is just a smattering of items that can either add to your wine-drinking enjoyment or waste your money.

The best source we've found for all things wine-related is www.wineenthusiast.com. Get on their mailing list and you'll never lack for wine paraphernalia again.

Here are some fun things to waste . . . uh, spend your money on:

Tannin removers. These devices, which go by the names of Perfect Sommelier or The Wine Clip, claim to use magnetic force to soften the tannins in very young wine. We admit that we haven't tried them, but that's because we don't feel like shelling out $50. We'd rather just age the wine (more on aging in Chapter 13).

Wine thermometers. These devices provide digital readouts for various wines, some from outside the bottle. They're cool, but unnecessary. Generally, serve a white wine fifteen minutes after taking it from the fridge, and a red wine fifteen minutes after putting it *into* the fridge.

Champagne recorkers. These are cool; for about $10, they keep the bubbles in the sparkling wine bubbly.

Wine savers. There are numerous options when it comes to "recorking" a bottle of wine so it doesn't spoil. To be honest, we usually just stick the cork back in, leave it on the counter or in the fridge, and finish it the

following night. We often find that red wines, in particular, benefit from this treatment. But if you're not a
daily wine drinker like we are, then you need something to keep the oxygen from turning your wine into
vinegar.

You can spend thousands on elaborate wine bottle
preservation systems, or just a few bucks on a small
device that pumps the oxygen out of the air. We recommend going with the simplest options—unless you're
drinking wine that costs hundreds of dollars a bottle.

Wine bags. These neoprene wine holders are great
for transporting your vino to a restaurant or a friend's
house for dinner. Buy a few; they have a tendency to
get left behind.

One thing that's not worth wasting your money on
are those fancy wine cleaning solutions you see in the
wine catalogs. Instead, just keep a bucket of the all-pur-
pose OxyClean handy. Nothing gets red wine stains out
of clothing, tablecloths, cloth napkins, or carpet any
better.

CHAPTER 13

AGING AND STORING WINE

*S*hould you age wine or should you swig it tonight? The answer depends.

First, forget about aging any wine that cost less than $25. Oh, sure, you can keep it around for a year or two, but not because it needs to age, simply because it may take you that long to drink the two cases you were coerced into buying at the fire sale at the local wine store. Conversely, the more the wine costs, the more likely it is that it will improve with age.

You can also forget about most whites, rosés, and light reds, such as Beaujolais and Grenache. They're ready for drinking here and now. You can store them for a year or two, but not much longer. They won't go bad; they'll just lose their freshness and appeal.

When it comes to reds—Shiraz, Zinfandel, Cabernet Sauvignon, Merlot, Burgundy, Pinot Noir— read the label. Many wineries will tell you if the wine will benefit from aging. Also check out reviews of the wine, either online or in wine magazines (just type the name and year of the wine into a search engine and see what comes up). People who know a lot more about

WINE DRINKERS ASK . . .
ARE ANY WHITE WINES WORTH AGING?

Yes, some white wines improve with age. Generally, higher-end white Burgundies (made from chardonnay grapes), Sauternes, some German wines, and the Tokay Pinot Gris from Alsace, France, are worth aging. You can even age good Champagne for ten years or more.

wine than you or we ever will post their thoughts about whether that wine would benefit from some time in the bottle.

Unless you're dealing with Barberas, Barolos, super Tuscans, vintage Ports, or very high-end Bordeaux—the type of wines that benefit from long-term storage (think ten years or more)—check your reds again after six to eight years.

We have another way to tell. We open the bottle, pour a glass, and sip it slowly all evening. If the wine improves as the night goes on, it will probably benefit from aging. Try the rest of the bottle the next night. Again, if the tannins have softened and the wine has "opened up," then you can be assured that letting it sit for a couple of years and trying it again is a good idea.

TRACKING YOUR WINE

If you're aging wine, you want to make sure you don't lose track of it. If you let it go too long, it will pass its prime and lose its depth, turning into a weak, shallow shadow of its former self.

To track what you've got stored, you can buy one of the many types of wine tracking software available (search online for "wine cellar software"). Many will even let you download a trial version.

But you really don't need fancy software. An Excel spreadsheet works just as well, particularly if you store your wine in wine racks, which are really just large grids. Keith matched every column and row of wine racks to a column and row in an Excel spreadsheet to keep track of his wine.

A less high-tech option is to use bottle labels. These erasable labels hang on the neck of the bottle and cost about $15 for 100. You can write where you bought the wine, how much it cost, when you began storing it, and when you think it's ready for drinking.

Now, as for where to store that wine: Although you don't have to get fancy, when it comes to storing more than a few bottles of wine for more than a few weeks, you should try to find a place with the following elements:

Consistent temperature. The ideal temperature for storing wine is considered to be 55 degrees. We're not sure how anyone actually came up with this temperature, and we have yet to see any scientific studies suggesting that storing the wine, say, five degrees higher or lower will significantly affect its quality. So figure anywhere between 50 and 60 degrees is fine. To us, the most important thing when it comes to temperature is coolness and consistency. The warmer the temperature, the faster the wine will age. So if you're seventy-five and still sitting on twelve cases of 2000 Bordeaux, you might want to turn up the heat just a bit so they're ready to drink in a year instead of another ten. But if most of your wine is for drinking in the next couple of years, or storing for the next decade or more, keep it cool. And keep it consistent. The main thing that hurts wine is big fluctuations in temperature (don't keep it in your unheated or non-air-conditioned garage).

Darkness. Just as ultraviolet light prematurely ages your skin, it can also prematurely age your wine, even wine stored in dark bottles. So keep the lights as dim as possible, particularly for sparkling wine, which is even more sensitive to light.

Humidity. The dampness that comes from a humid environment helps keep the corks from drying out, which could allow too much oxygen into the wine, prematurely aging it. Of course, you don't want too much dampness—you might lose the labels.

Calmness. If your neighbor on the other side of the wall where your wine is stored likes to blast his stereo so high you feel the vibrations in your apartment, move your wine. Vibrations and constant movement kicks up sediment in a red wine and could damage the wine.

Cleanliness. Don't store your wine in a fridge with stinky cheese or Brussels sprouts. Believe it or not, the odor can actually enter through the cork and harm the wine. And keep the area clean; junk and garbage invites bugs and fungus, neither of which you want near your precious hoard.

You should also have enough space to store your wine on its side. This keeps some liquid in constant contact with the cork and prevents the cork from drying out. Fortified wines, however, (except Port) should be stored standing up. And if your wine has sediment in it, stand it straight for a few days before drinking so the sediment sinks to the bottom.

As for turning bottles of wine on the racks, there's no need.

FINDING ROOM TO STORE THE WINE

A few years ago, when wine was simply something to end a hectic day, we rarely had more than six or seven bottles at a time in our house. We stored them in a countertop wine rack under the microwave. Then we got bitten by the wine bug. And suddenly *cases* of wine started turning up in the house.

Where, oh where, to put them?

Read on for some creative options for mere mortals like us who can't hire someone to build a solid-cherry, temperature-controlled, 2,000-bottle wine room complete with humidification and tile floors.

Look down. If you're lucky enough to live in an area of the country where the houses have cellars, you're golden. Basements are the ideal storage place for wine, particularly the unfinished section of the basement. They tend to stay a consistent temperature, are usually dark, and the dampness provides just the right level of humidity. You can buy some inexpensive wine racks (see Resources) and line an outside wall with them, then just pop your bottles in. Or you can get a bit more ambitious and do what we did: build a simple "room" around the racks.

That's what Keith and our then-thirteen-year-old son did in a weekend. They framed out three walls around the outer wall of the cellar, covered it with two sheets of drywall sandwiching a plug of super-efficient insulation, and then added a thick door and a lock (we have teenagers, after all). That's it! The insulation kept the little "room" cooler than even the surrounding basement, and Keith got to brag about his "wine cellar."

Look under. Under beds and cabinets, for instance. They're dark, out of the way, not likely to have a lot of vibrations (depending on what happens on the bed itself). You can raise the bed with bed risers sold at home stores to provide more storage room. Then lay the wine side by side in those under-bed plastic storage boxes. They're easy to pull out to see what you have and select the evening's wine. We don't really recommend this for aging fine wine, but it works great for storing all that wine you've started buying now that you've read this book.

Look up. Again, not ideal for storing fine wine meant to age—but great for storing plain ol' drinking wine—are the spaces above kitchen counters, the tops of credenzas and armoires, and so on. You can buy small wine racks that hold six to a dozen bottles and stick them up high. Twine a few fake grape leaves through it and you've now got yourself a decorating accessory (as well the evening's libation).

Plug it in. Say you've decided you're ready to invest in some wines worth aging. But say you live in a one-room apartment in Manhattan and have nowhere to store it. Never fear. For about $100, you can get a sleek wine refrigerator about the size of a microwave that holds up to sixteen bottles. If you're willing to invest a bit more, you can store fifty bottles for under $400. You can also get larger wine coolers that store more than 500 bottles at a time, many of which come with three different temperature zones for red, white, and rosé. The coolers are designed to protect your wine from light and vibrations, just like a real cellar. And if you're really tight on space, just plug them into any outlet (including the bedroom), throw a pretty scarf or cloth over it, and voila! instant furniture.

And that's just the tip of the proverbial iceberg. Commercial wine storage centers will store your wine and ship it to you when you want/need it. We've also seen high-end apartment buildings that offer wine storage—complete with computerized tracking systems and video cameras so you can virtually "visit" your wine.

As for us, well, when we moved from Pennsylvania to Virginia we lost our lovely basement with its self-regulating wine room. The new house had no basement. But it did have an unfinished space under the eaves off our office. We hired a carpenter to build a room within

DON'T MAKE THIS MISTAKE

Here's what *not* to do: Don't store your good wine in the regular fridge. Not only will the odors from the food seep into the bottle, but the constantly low temperature will kill the wine.

the room, installed a compressor to maintain a constant temperature and humidity, tiled the floor, added a super-insulated door, and set up the racks. The kids call it "Daddy's happy place," and yes, Keith is a happy man when he's in the 55-degree room perusing his wine.

WRAPPING IT ALL UP

So how do you feel about wine now? Ready to pop the cork on a bottle of Merlot rather than pulling the tab on a can of beer? We hope so. We hope that, like us, you will find your passion for all things wine ignited, and feel ready to start on the wonderful journey of wine.

But don't take our word for it. Head out on your own path. Pick up a wine you've never heard of, subscribe to a wine-related magazine (see Resources for some ideas), plan a wine-related trip, or just visit a winery in your area. No matter what you do, keep an open mind. Remember our golden rule: There are no rules. If you open a bottle you don't like, set it aside and use it for cooking or just pour it down the drain. If you love it, order a case. Try wines that cost $5 and wines that cost $50. Drink it in paper cups and in fine crystal.

Just never stop experimenting and learning. And hey, do us one other favor: Once you become truly passionate about wine, spread the word. Personally, we think the more wine lovers there are in the world, the better the world will be.

Cheers!

RESOURCES

Have we whetted your appetite for all things wine? Here's a short list with a few additional resources. Don't stop here, though; you can find thousands of books, Web sites, blogs, and so forth, devoted to this endlessly interesting topic.

BOOKS

Clarke, Oz. *Oz Clark's Encyclopedia of Grapes*. New York: Harcourt, Inc. 2001. This is a very detailed book about all of the major grape varieties and more.

MacNeil, Karen. *The Wine Bible*. New York: Workman Publishing, 2001. A very readable and enjoyable 900-plus page voyage through the world of wine.

Zraly, Kevin. *Windows on the World Complete Wine Course*. New York: Sterling Publishing Co., Inc. 2004. A thorough introduction to wine by one of the best respected educators in the business.

MAGAZINES

Decanter. (800) 875-2997, www.decanter.com. The leading wine magazine in the United Kingdom.

Quarterly Review of Wines. www.QRW.com. For those who *want* to know wines, from those who do.

The Wine Advocate. (410) 329-6477, www.eRobertParker.com. Robert Parker's consumers guide. A densely packed newsletter filled with detailed tasting notes on hundreds of wines.

Wine Enthusiast. (800) 829-5901, www.winemag.com. One of two must-have wine magazines for wine lovers in the United States. Lots of wine reviews, food stories, travel stories.

Wine Spectator. (800) 752-7799, www.winespectator.com. The other must-have. This publication is very similar to the *Wine Enthusiast*.

The World of Fine Wine. www.finewinemag.com. In-depth articles on wine for the true connoisseur.

WEB SITES

www.jancisrobinson.com. Homepage for wine writer and educator Jancis Robinson. Some free content and members-only detailed tasting notes, and more.

www.windowswineschool.com. Web site for *Windows on the World Complete Wine Course,* the book mentioned earlier.

www.winepricex.com. An online wine valuation and inventory management service with commercial trading features.

WINE STORES

Pop's Wines & Spirits. 256 Long Beach Rd.,
Island Park, NY 11558, (516) 431-0025 (phone),
(516) 432-2648 (fax), www.popswine.com. Large
inventory, catalogs, and periodic special offerings.
Shipping where allowed.

Premier Cru. 5890 Christie Ave., Emeryville, CA
94608, (510) 655-6691 (phone), (510) 547-5405
(fax), www.premiercru.net. Periodic offerings of
fine wines. Most as futures (pre-arrival offerings),
have to pay when you order and wait for
shipments to come in. Shipping where allowed.

Southern Hemisphere Wine Center. 5973
Engineer Dr., Huntington Beach, CA 92649,
(800) 504-9463 (toll free), (714) 892-6930 (fax),
www.southernwines.com. A great store to pick up
bargains on New World wines. Occasional e-mail
offers and catalogs. Shipping where allowed.

Wine Library. 586 Morris Ave., Springfield, NJ 07081,
(973) 376-0005 (phone), (888) 980-WINE
(toll free), www.winelibrary.com. A well-marketed
full-service wine store with almost daily special
offers and shipping (where allowed).

ORGANIZATIONS

American Wine Society. P.O. Box 3330, Durham,
NC 27702, (919) 403-0022 (phone), (919)
403-0392 (fax), www.americanwinesociety.org.

OTHER WINE RESOURCES

55 Degrees. 1210 Church St., St. Helena, CA 94574,
    (707) 963-5513 (phone), (707) 963-5281 (fax),
    www.fiftyfivedegrees.com. A temperature-
    controlled wine storage facility that rents out
    storage space in the heart of the Napa Valley.
    Allows you to consolidate local wine offerings.

INDEX